Denying the Deniers

A Soldier's Intersection with the Holocaust

John Regnier

With Susan T. Hessel

D.B. Reinhart Institute for Ethics in Leadership

Viterbo University
La Crosse, Wisconsin

Printed in the United States of America

ISBN 978-0-9816896-8-5

D.B. Reinhart Institute for Ethics in Leadership
Viterbo University
900 Viterbo Drive
La Crosse, WI 54601
www.viterbo.edu/ethics

D.B. REINHART INSTITUTE *for* ETHICS IN LEADERSHIP *at* VITERBO UNIVERSITY

The D.B. Reinhart Institute for Ethics in Leadership is located on the campus of Viterbo University in La Crosse, Wisconsin. Its mission is to promote the concept of ethics in leadership as integral to the advancement of American society and to advance leadership and ethics through publications, courses, conferences, workshops, and public forums.

To my dear wife and partner of 63 years,
EVA MAE (CANN) REGNIER,
who died on December 27, 2012.

She contributed greatly to my post-war life through
the wonderful things that we did together
as a couple and family.

Eva Mae also assisted greatly in developing and keeping track
of my World War II experiences. This book would
have been much harder without her efforts
in preserving the letters and my diary.
My only regret is she is not here
to appreciate this book
she so encouraged
me to write over
the years.

CONTENTS

The things I saw beggar description. . . . The visual evidence and the verbal testimony of starvation, cruelty, and bestiality were so overpowering as to leave me a bit sick. In one room, where there were piled 20 to 30 naked men killed by starvation. General Patton would not even enter. He said he would get sick if he did so. I made the visit deliberately, in order to be in a position to give firsthand evidence of these things if ever, in the future, there develops a tendency to charge these allegations merely to propaganda.[1]

—General Dwight D. Eisenhower

PREFACE

By Darryle Clott

As a Holocaust educator at Viterbo University in La Crosse, Wisconsin, I am fortunate to know many survivors who greatly enriched my life. Missing in my study of the Holocaust was interviewing a concentration camp liberator.

In April 2010 I wrote a letter to the editor of the *La Crosse Tribune* asking if there were World War II veterans who had liberated any of the camps and would be willing to meet with me. A friend, Sister Dolores Henke, called me and said she knew the perfect veteran for me to interview, but we would have to travel to Stevens Point, Wisconsin, where he lived. She offered to go with my husband, Marv, and me to visit John Regnier and his wife, Eva Mae. Little did I know that our visit would result in a beautiful friendship and, eventually, this book.

John was 89 at the time, but his memories were as fresh as if they had happened the day before. John still recalls exact details of entering Ohrdruf—the first camp liberated by the U.S. Army, calling this subcamp of the Buchenwald Concentration Camp "hell on earth" and the most terrible sight he had ever seen. His battalion had stumbled on the camp when then U.S. General Dwight Eisenhower was about to enter it along with Generals Patton and Bradley. Eisenhower, wanting the world to know the truth, instructed soldiers who had cameras to take photos so the world could never deny the atrocities committed there.

John and his buddy shared a camera and took photos, which he willingly shared with me along with many letters he had written home about his experiences. He also showed me the war diary he kept.

Marv and I fell in love with John and Eva Mae at that initial meeting, and that admiration has only grown. They are one of my favorite couples I've met in my life. To spend time with them is to be surrounded by love.

I went home that night with pages and pages of notes and the many photos and stories John had given me. I was determined to organize them in an effective way to share with my classes at Viterbo. They remained untouched until Rick Kyte, Director of Ethics in Leadership at Viterbo, received a call from Sean Van Domelen, a young high school student who was looking for a project to do on World War II, especially something Holocaust-related. Rick, with whom I work to bring in survivors as speakers, asked me if I had an idea for Sean. I replied, "Do I ever have an idea!"

I accompanied Sean and his parents to Stevens Point to interview John in June of 2011. Sean did an extraordinary project, the creation of a documentary on John's experience at Ohrdruf. In March 2012, both Sean and John presented at the Holocaust Educators' Workshop at Viterbo. As usual, everyone who met them fell in love with John and Eva Mae.

I decided that the time had come for John's story to be written, so I went to my friend Susan T. Hessel, a personal historian who is dedicated to preserving life stories of individuals. Sue wrote *Squirrel Is Alive: A Teenager in the Belgian Resistance and French Underground* about my dear friend Mary Rostad, who worked in the resistance against the Nazis as a young woman in Belgium and France. I knew I could trust Sue to do an outstanding job with John's story. So back I went to Stevens Point with Sue to meet John in May 2013. I am amazed at Sue's remarkable ability to take voluminous pages of information and weave it together into a narrative I do not want to end.

She has done it again! I see Mary and John's stories as bookends in Holocaust literature. John's story is another gift to Holocaust educators and those interested in the Holocaust and WWII. Susan not only gives us John's story of entering a concentration camp but his experiences as a young soldier during WWII. One can read about the statistics, facts, and figures of war, but it is not until one reads the personal accounts that it comes alive for us. We appreciate the extreme challenges and difficulties our veterans experienced and how much we owe them. The story you are about to read is not only about the war, it is a love story and one of faith.

The only sadness for me is that John's beloved Eva Mae died December 27, 2012. Upon the wedding of our son Hans, who recently married at age 41, John sent me a note saying, "Although your son held out for a long time, he apparently found the perfect partner. I can identify somewhat because I completed my WWII service and college (age 28) before I found my perfect partner, Eva Mae. My life is very different after our 63 years together, but I have to accept her passing, as she would want me to do. My faith, a very fine and helpful family, many wonderful friends, including you and Marv, and great memories of our life together, make it possible to carry on."

Carry on indeed, dear friend!

DENYING THE DENIERS

INTRODUCTION

An Intersection with History

The war in Europe was rapidly coming to its end—although certainly not as quickly as many millions dreamed, including myself. And certainly the war in the Pacific was a constant worry. The men of my Army unit already were warned to prepare for the invasion of Japan after our work in Europe was done.

Our medical battalion, assigned to provide medical support to the 3rd Army's Fourth Armored Division, was on the road in Germany in April 1945 when our commanding officer, Colonel Francis R. Sandford spotted troops assembled just outside the village of Ohrdruf near Gotha, Germany, which was about 12 to 15 miles west of Buchenwald, a place we did not know about at the time. He led our convoy off the road to learn what was going on.

It potentially was a matter of our safety. While the Nazis were in retreat, pockets of the fierce Schutzstaffel (SS) troops remained behind the lines as snipers. They were known to don uniforms of dead U.S. soldiers to get close enough to pick us off. We always worried that we would be next, especially at night, although we did feel there was safety in numbers.

We noticed an Army jeep with five stars, which Colonel Sandford said had to be General Dwight D. Eisenhower's,

Supreme Allied Commander in Europe (and eventually our 34th U.S. president). When we were motioned to join the other assembled soldiers, we found ourselves at an intersection with history with even more top brass. With Eisenhower were the famous General George S. Patton, Jr. of the 3rd Army and General Omar Bradley, commander of all U.S. ground forces invading Germany—1.3 million. Also present was General Walton Walker, who was a general under Patton during World War II and later head of the 8th Army in Korea before his death in 1950 when he tried to pass a column of stalled Southern Korean Army vehicles near Seoul.

A unit of Patton's 3rd Army was the first to stumble on and liberate the Ohrdruf slave labor camp, near the village of Ohrdruf. And it was a stumble. Historians tell us that Patton's men were not searching for a slave labor camp; they were seeking a secret Nazi communications center that the U.S. Army feared was related to German atomic warfare research.

What that unit found in this camp at Ohrdruf was so horrifying that Generals Eisenhower and Bradley toured the camp with General Patton. And, as it turned out, this camp was mild compared to some others discovered by American and other Allied soldiers on an almost daily basis as they moved through Germany east of the Rhine. The Russians also were liberating camps as they moved west. They found extermination camps: Chelmno, Belzec, Sobibor, Treblinka, Auschwitz-Birkenau, and Majdanek.

What is the difference between a concentration camp, a

slave labor camp, and an extermination camp? The Germans, I later learned, considered concentration camps to be places where political prisoners were confined, usually for a long period of time; slave camps were where prisoners were forced to work long hours for the German war effort; and death camps were designed for "The Final Solution": the systematic extermination of Jews and others considered undesirable in society. Most Americans only heard the term concentration camp for decades.

On that day in Ohrdruf, we saw and heard Eisenhower expressing shock at what we all saw. He wanted many witnesses, urging anyone with a camera to take photographic evidence. As Ike later wrote, "I made the visit deliberately, in order to be in a position to give firsthand evidence of these things if ever, in the future, there develops a tendency to charge these allegations merely to propaganda."[2]

I shared a camera with Technical Sgt. Fred Kercheval, another Midwesterner with whom I served, beginning in basic training. We recorded what our minds could not believe—deliberately starved corpses stacked like cordwood on impromptu incinerators designed to hide the evidence of so many dead at Nazi hands. Photos taken by ordinary soldiers like us also documented thousands of bodies buried in huge pits and unburied in "body sheds," a place where corpses were stored until they could be turned into ashes. They were all sprinkled with quick lime, unsuccessful attempts to disguise the sickening terrible odor that for miles ahead of any camp signaled death and plenty of it.

While I had never been on the front lines of battle, the horrors of war already came to us in the form of thousands of wounded soldiers—American and German—who were treated in the hospital to which our medical battalion was assigned. But nothing prepared us for what we saw in that camp.

As I wrote to my family, "After leaving the concentration camp, it was still hard for me to believe what I had seen, and that it all occurred such a short time before our seeing it. Life was so cheap in that hell-hole."[3]

General Dwight D. Eisenhower visiting the slave-labor camp at Ohrdruf, Germany, on April 12, 1945. My friend, Fred Kercheval, is just behind General Eisenhower's left shoulder. The General's head is blocking mine in the photo. (National Archives.)

I will describe more about the images of the dead that remain indelible in my mind 70-plus years later. I was an ordinary soldier who found myself at the intersection of what became known as the Holocaust, something I knew so little about before that meeting beside the road. As a non-com, a technical sergeant, I had an unprecedented opportunity to stand beside giants in the Army on that April day in 1945.

When you are an enlisted soldier, you do not know the "big picture" of war, only what you are told and experience yourself. Much of what you will read in this book combines my memories with additional sources that I later read and studied.

I was silent for many decades about my experience, but when I hear some claim the Holocaust never happened, I must speak up. I am forever grateful to have the photographic proof, my wartime diary, and letters that I wrote home during that period. I am fortunate that my mother saved them for me, along with historic newspapers that I mailed home.

With this book, I am denying the deniers. I was there. I witnessed evidence of the "cruelest uncivilized murders that the world has ever seen." And it occurred, I wrote in my April 16, 1945 letter home, in "a nice, quiet little village along one of the main highways with the sun shining down on the green grass and rolling hills in the adjacent areas. One would never dream that dozens of starved and lime-devoured corpses lay only a short distance from the town in the concentration camp."

CHAPTER ONE

From the Beginning

I also grew up on a farm near a "nice, quiet little village"—the southwestern Minnesota town of Cottonwood. It was just north of Marshall, the big town in the area with a population of 4,590 in 1940. Cottonwood and Marshall were not so unlike Ohrdruf except for the very obvious. No community is perfect, but ours had no hidden evil that citizens pretended they didn't know existed.

The village of my youth was composed of hard-working farm people—many of whom traced their life there back to the U.S. Homestead Act, which helped settle "the West." The 1862 Act, signed by Abraham Lincoln, promised 160 acres at little or no cost for those who staked out a claim farming or ranching land out West. It was open to anyone age 21 or older, including former slaves. Some 270 million acres of land—about 10 percent of the country—were inhabited as a result of this act.

The U.S. government did this because settlements were needed across the country to warrant development of the cross-continental railroad that eventually connected our two coasts. Unless sufficient people lived on the prairies on the way to the West Coast, railroad builders saw no reason to expand.

The family of my dad, Oscar Arthur Regnier, came from France originally and then immigrated to Canada before moving to New England for a time. They then lived in Kankakee, Illinois, where many other French people lived. The final move was to land near Marshall in Lyon County, Minnesota, although other relatives went even farther west to Kansas and Nebraska. Over time, my grandfather, John Baptist Regnier, added other land parcels that he purchased from other farmers. The land where my grandfather and his wife, Severine, raised their family eventually reached about 400 to 500 acres.

My mother, Nellie Boyd (Christensen) Regnier, was born in the United States to Christopher and Anna Christensen. Christopher and his brother James decided to come to the United States with their wives to avoid lengthy Army conscription in their native Denmark. They homesteaded successfully in Lyon County in Minnesota. We had such a close relationship with Uncle Jim that we kids came to think of him as our grandfather, not uncle. We didn't see as much of our actual grandfather because of limited transportation in those days.

My mother, the first born in the family, had just finished the sixth grade when her mother died in childbirth of their fifth child, a boy named Warner William Christensen. With this infant and three other siblings—a sister and two brothers—her father had no choice but have Nellie drop out of school at age 12 to care for her siblings.

Even more challenging, Warner developed rheumatic fever as a two year old. She cared for him in those last months before he died. My mother told me that many people thought then that children didn't grieve, but it was not true. She loved that little boy and mourned for him all her life.

I don't have the details, but father and mother met because their farms were not so far from each other in country terms, about two to three miles apart. They married on July 18, 1916, and went on to have ten children, all of whom graduated from Marshall High School. That was an incredible feat then—even newsworthy in the local paper when the last of my siblings, Dean, received a diploma—because high school was anything but expected in my parents' days. My dad finished eighth grade and my mom sixth, but their learning did not end when they left school. They were self-taught after they left their formal education and were committed to the education of their ten children.

After my grandfather left the farm and bought a house in Marshall, my father, Oscar, and his brother Henry each rented farms in Lyon County, Minnesota, which they farmed for many years.

My parents' first son was named after my mother's brother, although he became known as William Warner, rather than Warner William, and was called Bill. I was the fourth child in the family, born October 15, 1921, however my birth certificate mistakenly showed the 14th. Recognizing I would have problems getting the GI Bill after World War II if my birth certificate did not match my Army records, the county register of deeds pulled out a pen and changed my birth certificate from

My paternal grandmother, Severine, and paternal grandfather, Jean Baptiste Regnier.

My maternal grandmother, Anna, and maternal grandfather, Christopher Christensen, with their first four children: my mother, Nellie, her brother Fritz, and sitting in front of him is Marie. Christopher holds baby George.

Clockwise from top: Emil (Chick); Oscar, my dad; Pete (the Green Bay Packer player); and Hank, seated.

Top to bottom: my father's sisters, Ollie, Sis, and Edna, seated.

the 14th to the 15th. These were very different times.

One of my earliest memories is of my grandfather John Baptist Regnier dying in 1927. Wakes were held in the parlor, with the tradition of someone staying with the body 24 hours a day until burial. I tagged along with my dad one night when it was his duty to spend the night with him. It was the first time I had seen a casket or someone who had died. I don't remember being scared; it was more like feeling proud to be old enough to be in on this tradition. I probably slept a bit at my grandparents' house, maybe on a couch in another room. Why me? I probably knew Dad was going and asked to go with him. I was certainly a curious kid.

I often was the one who went with Dad when he went into town. Again, maybe I was the only available kid at the time and the others were busy. But I remember riding in a horse and buggy to town, where my dad visited the implement dealer. I played in the waiting room with toy tractors and implements while Dad took care of his business. I wish I had those toys today.

My Childhood

Like so many farm families, the Regnier kids attended a one-room country school—the District 90 School in Lyon County—which was between Cottonwood and Marshall. All eight grades were in the same classroom, which meant we always heard previews of what we would learn in future years. Students all got along and learned from each other.

Our farm was the closest one to the school, so it was convenient for my mother to offer a room in our own house to the teacher. My mother was on the school board, serving as treasurer, which meant she handled the books and paid the teacher. Being on the school board was significant, considering she only had that 6th grade education.

We shared the upstairs with our teacher, who had to live with a bunch of rambunctious kids. I can remember several of us sneaking into the teacher's room—the big one upstairs—so we could get dressed in her closet, which was much warmer than our room because the chimney went from the living room to the upstairs through her room. We waited, of course, for her to leave for school to enter that closet. Teachers then did a little of everything in one-room schools, including getting the stove started before students arrived so we had heat.

I was not always a fan of my teachers; at least not a fan of one of them. When I was in the second grade, art suddenly was in the curriculum. Each school, including mine, received a bucket of clay from which we were to sculpt something. Living on a farm, I chose to sculpt a horse and was very proud of what I made. My teacher took one look at my anatomically-correct horse and then slammed her fist down on my artwork to crush it. For good measure, she clubbed my knuckles with her ruler. I didn't understand why she hated my sculpture: that's what a horse looked like on our farm.

I steamed and plotted my revenge all the way home. I raided my father's workbench for nails and a hammer and went to work in the outhouse, pounding nails around the "hole" this teacher used at our house. We kids used a smaller one in that same outhouse, and I didn't think about other innocent adults getting hurt from my act of revenge. Luckily, my mother spotted what I had done before harm was done to my teacher—or anyone else—and made me remove the nails. I reeled with the weight of injustice because that darn teacher had ruined my horse.

This teacher later married and lived on a neighboring farm, becoming friends with my folks. One day, my kind and compassionate parents saw a "quarantine" sign on this teacher's property, which meant no one could go inside because of measles or some other childhood disease. Worried that they would not have enough food to last through the quarantine, my parents put together a box of groceries, which they left at the gate. My parents probably called the family to tell them the groceries were there, since they could not go on the actual property.

That was the era of the country phone or party line, in which multiple families shared a telephone line. We all knew each other's ring—ours was one long followed by two shorts. That was supposed to keep others on the line from picking up the wrong call, but "rubberneckers," as they were called, loved to listen in on other people's conversations. Rubbernecking was often more efficient for spreading news, including health problems, than the newspaper.

Family Members of Some Note

My dad's family had two members from his generation who received regional attention. Uncle Pete Regnier left his new dental practice in 1922 to play a season with the new Green Bay Packers football team, formed in 1921. A standout player while at the University of Minnesota, Uncle Pete was recruited into a practice game with other Minnesota players against the Packers before the 1922 season began. He played both quarterback and halfback in an era in which players played both offense and defense—and wore very little protective and quite primitive equipment in the game.

Uncle Pete must have played quite well against the Packers, because he was asked to join the team that season. My Aunt Olivine (Ollie) told the story of how Uncle Pete once came on the train to Marshall after a game with the Packers. He was so black and blue that he sat in a hot tub for a couple of hours to ease his many aches and pains. After the bath, he was loosened up and able to move much more.

After that one season, Uncle Pete decided he was better off practicing dentistry than playing professional football. I remember occasions when Uncle Pete threw the football to us when he and his friends came out to Marshall for pheasant hunting. We kids could see he was quite good. Sadly, he died of cancer at age 42 in 1938.

My dad's youngest brother, Emil, whom we called Uncle Chick, was active in Minnesota politics. He served in the Min-

My Uncle Pete was a University of Minnesota football player. His experience with the Minnesota Gophers led to a pickup game with what was then known as the Acme Packers. After this pickup game, he was offered a job in 1922 with the Packers, because the team was so impressed with his abilities. The Packers are now known, of course, as the Green Bay Packers.

nesota Senate from 1931 to 1934 as a member of the Farmer-Labor Party, which was comparable to the Progressive Party in Wisconsin and the Nonpartisan Liberal League in North Dakota. Founded with the help of Governor Floyd Olson, the Farmer-Labor Party was dominant in Minnesota during the Great Depression. In 1943, Governor Elmer Benson, Hubert Humphrey, and Eugenie Moore Anderson successfully convinced his party to merge with the Democratic Party to become the Democratic-Farmer-Labor Party (DFL).

Uncle Chick's Minnesota Senate career included working to end mandatory Reserved Officers Training Corps (ROTC) at the University of Minnesota and to pass the amendment to repeal Prohibition.[4] I'm sure my uncle, like so many Americans, had grown tired of the crime, gangs, and racketeering that followed the ban on alcohol in the United States. Our family members were never heavy drinkers, but they did enjoy beer, which my Uncle Hank produced quietly on his farm. Federal agents were not so interested in the home brewers. They wanted the big players in illegal alcohol production and sales, the ones profiting on illegal alcohol sales.

After Calvin Coolidge was elected president in 1924, Uncle Chick wrote a letter to his sister, Ollie, that illustrated his feelings about that election. From that letter, it is clear that Uncle Emil did not mince words. He wrote it like he saw it. Noting the Ku Klux Klan had endorsed Coolidge, he wrote,

> *Boy oh boy, if I could ever be a lawyer, I'd specialize in the work of fighting the common people's battles against the privileged interests, such as the Standard Oil Co. and all the railroads. It makes me so mad to see the damn crooks pose as gentlemen and they are lowest type of mankind living. . . .*
>
> *Here is one thing that makes my blood boil. The Republican machine started the false propaganda that LaFollette was against our parochial schools and against the homes. Isn't that rot? Our good Catholics accepted this as the truth and voted for Cal Coolidge who was endorsed by the Klan. It is no wonder that this was a Republican landslide. Our good priests instructed the*

people the Sunday prior to Election Day not to vote for the third party, but to vote for Republicans. How's that for well organized political machine? They had the endorsement of the Klan and the Catholics voted side by side with their great opposition. What would you rather have as Pres, a man who has publicly condemned the Klan or one who will sue the Government to further the ambitions of that rotten invisible empire? A few more years of rule by the reactionaries and America will blush with shame at its ignorance, for our great free country will no longer be a free one but will be controlled by the money bags of Wall Street. . . .

I'm a stronger radical than I was before the election. That briefly tells you my political beliefs. I say radical, for that is what they call us. However, we are not radical but progressive.

Uncle Chick ran the 1930 gubernatorial campaign for Floyd Olson, who served in that office from January 6, 1931, until he died from stomach cancer on August 22, 1935. After his death, Uncle Chick was pressured to run for governor, but he declined.

My uncle became the staff person for the successful campaign of Magnus Johnson in 1932 for the U.S. House of Representatives, where he served through 1935. Johnson had served in the U.S. Senate from Minnesota from July 16, 1923, to March 4, 1925, but lost his bid for re-election in 1924. Johnson also ran unsuccessfully for Minnesota Governor in 1936, the year he died.

Campaigning in the 1930s meant either a half-hour speech on the radio or weekend farm rallies that were very well attended. Although I sometimes went with my father to rallies, Dad and I missed the one that became a great part of Regnier family lore. My uncle told me the story, however, about the Sunday afternoon when he and the candidate arrived an hour early to check out the landscape for the rally. Discovering the farmer's yard was absolutely flat, they realized the candidate would be lost in the crowd of listeners if the 1,000 or so expected came there.

Magnus asked the farmer if he had a hayrack or wagon that he could stand on. "Golly, I don't," the farmer responded, "But I have a manure spreader back of the barn."

That would do.

My uncle introduced Magnus, who did indeed stand on the manure spreader. He immediately won over the crowd when he said, "I'm very pleased to have the first opportunity ever to speak from the Republican platform." He then went on to talk for an hour and a half.

The Great Depression

Of course, that speech was given in the midst of the Great Depression, a time of national suffering during my childhood years. Times were so rough that they radicalized ordinary people who just wanted to make a living. Dad and his brothers talked about the seriousness of our problems, particularly for farmers who received so little for their long, backbreaking labor after prices dropped so dramatically. It was hardly worth selling their crops and animals if they got back less than the cost of producing the nation's food.

Most frustrating were the middlemen, who seemed to make big profits while the farmers suffered and lost their land. Business people picked up foreclosed farms for very little, leaving the former owners to try to squeak by as renters.

Irate farmers formed the Farmers Holiday Association, which urged members to destroy crops rather than practically give them away. The association, trying to prevent foreclosures any way they could, demanded farmers be paid for crops and livestock based on their actual costs of production, not just what the market would bear. As part of their strikes in 1932, they blocked roads to farms that were being auctioned off after foreclosure. Others demonstrated anger and frustration by burning crops and pouring milk into fields. They did so in the hope that shortages would follow, leading to higher prices because demand would exceed supply.

My parents never joined these groups, though they understood the fear and despondency that led to them. Farmers feared the life they loved would literally and figuratively blow away.

Chick, then in the Minnesota Senate, was so highly respected by both farmers and businessmen that he was asked to mediate near-riot conditions around a Marshall meatpacking plant where farmers stood with pitchforks and firearms.

Uncle Chick told businessmen that he needed something to offer the farmers. After receiving a concession from the business leaders, Chick stood on a hayrack to tell protestors that the owners agreed to a temporary plant closing. That eased the very tense situation enough to get the farmers to go home.

My dad and his brothers often said our country might have gone the way of the Russian revolution if it were not for the U.S. Constitution, our public school system, and an electoral system that provided the ability to vote folks out of office.

As rough as it was for farmers, in some ways they were better off than those living in cities. At least with land, farmers could grow food to feed their families. Those in cities who were without work were more likely to go hungry. Despair was contagious in those days.

I used to overhear my folks speaking with great compassion at night about how difficult it was for some people. There was no formal support system then like we have now. Instead, Lyon County might provide families with a box of food or maybe shoes or clothes for the children. In exchange for that modest help, recipients were listed in the newspaper each month on the County Poor List. It was probably a way to shame them so they wouldn't ask for more. My parents always hoped that no one they knew would be on that list, as it seemed so unfair to them.

Some farmers in the country suffered even more during

the Great Depression, depending where they lived. Those who lived in the area that became known as the Dust Bowl—Oklahoma, Texas, and Kansas—watched their crops, animals, and dreams literally blown away by huge storms. Ours was nothing like the devastating experiences in the Dust Bowl, but we still had dust that piled up against fences like snow does in winter. I remember one such storm after school one day when I came home to learn my brother Bob was born. I went out in the midst of that blizzard of dust to tell the good news to my dad, who was working in the field.

In those other states, dust storms were relentless huge black clouds that turned the day into night. They destroyed crops, killed animals, and too often the very young and the very old and sometimes those in between from what became known as dust pneumonia. With no ability to earn money on their farms during those years, many banks foreclosed on property leaving the occupants no place to go. Many, particularly from Oklahoma, headed west to California, where they were not eagerly received. In fact, some Californians stood at the border with weapons to prevent their entry into the state. "They did not find a warm reception. Briefly in 1936 the Los Angeles police established a 'bum blockade' at the California borders to keep out undesirables."[5] It was the kind of experience that John Steinbach wrote about in his novel, *The Grapes of Wrath.*

A combination of natural causes and human folly created the dust storms. For years after World War I, farmers made big profits from wheat sales to other countries. They plowed up prairies to plant grain, whose prices rose dramatically in World War I. The land was uncovered as millions of acres that once provided natural grass cover were turned into cropland. After the United States suffered a devastating drought between the years from 1934 to 1937, there were no natural grasses or moisture to hold down the land. Dust from places like Texas traveled by the wind as far as the Atlantic Ocean. It is just an unbelievable concept today, although some places still have dust storms, just not as severe as in the 1930s.

Homes had very little insulation in those days because energy was so cheap and houses were built differently, not as tight as we have them today. That meant dust accumulated inside, requiring cleaning multiple times a day with dirt piled up in inches overnight. There was no relief from this suffering.

Not everyone suffered in the Depression; and some of those who did not had absolutely no sympathy for those who struggled. I heard from the mother of my best childhood friend about a doctor in Marshall who used to brag about reaching his life's ambition of setting up million dollar trust funds for each of his three kids. That would be equal to about $16.8 million each in 2012 dollars.[6]

What makes that bragging so appalling is that one day in the early 1930s my brother who was very sick went to that doctor, who diagnosed Bill as having an acute appendicitis. The doctor said Bill needed an immediate appendectomy to save his life, but would not do so unless my parents paid $100 in advance, about $1,680 in 2012 dollars. My parents were hardworking people who clearly did not have that kind of money; very few would in those times. Would this doctor just leave my brother to die? Yes. He was that heartless.

Fortunately, my Aunt Olivine (Ollie) worked as the nurse for another doctor in Marshall, Dr. Gastone Jacquot, an ears, nose, throat, and eyes specialist who previously had a family practice. Aunt Ollie had earned her diploma in a nursing program in Kankakee, Illinois, the city where the Regnier families lived before my grandfather and his brothers moved to the Marshall area.

Dr. Jacquot agreed to see Bill, having him stay in his offices over night with Aunt Ollie by his side. By morning, Bill had recovered enough to go home with his appendix intact. That other cruel, selfish doctor had even diagnosed my brother incorrectly. Bill did eventually have his appendix out, but it was at least a decade later while he was stationed in Italy in the Army during World War II.

Dr. Jacquot had a family practice in another town before he went back to Northwestern University in Evanston, Illinois, to get his specialty training. He cared for our entire family for all sorts of medical problems, and I don't think he ever sent my parents a bill. He was a model of compassion in medicine, not just for ours, but also for all families in his care.

The cruel doctor was not the only heartless person during those difficult times. One day, the landlord for the farm my father rented stopped by to check out our crops when it was harvest time. This landlord was one of those people who picked up farms for a pittance during the Great Depression. The only choice for the farmer whose land was foreclosed upon was to become a tenant farmer or find a job in town, where there were few available. Tenant farmers paid their rent by giving the landlord a third of the proceeds from each year's crops.

Our landlord kept a close eye on our crops to make sure he received his share, stopping by periodically to inspect them. At some point my father told him he'd need to hire someone to help with the harvesting.

"How old are those boys?" the landlord asked my father about my older brothers Billy and Jim.

"They will be going to high school so they won't be here to harvest the corn," my dad said.

"You should keep those boys right here," the landlord said. "There's no reason for them to go to high school."

That night I heard my mother and father talking in the kitchen, which was near our bedroom. "They have to go to high school," my mother said with determination. "We were not able to go, but these boys will go to high school."

My father agreed with Mom. They believed education was the way to a better future, even though the boys would still work on the farm as well as study. My mother valued the education she missed when her mother's death forced her to leave school after sixth grade to care for her younger siblings. Despite their limited formal education, my parents were well read and very bright, self-educated people.

Planning for My Future

Even though we always had food on our table, money was tight. We kids knew if we wanted to have education after high school, we had to pay for it ourselves. I earned $1.50 a week working Saturdays beginning at age 16 at Economy Grocery in Marshall. Brothers-in-law Frank Fielder and Henry Jolfs owned the store jointly.

As their Saturday helper, I delivered grocery orders, or I did whatever else needed to be done at the store, which remained open on Saturday nights because that was when farmers did their week's shopping.

An odd thing happened during my tenure with the store. I had an accident in which I broke a toe, which made me unable to work for about six weeks. The owners graciously filed a Worker's Compensation claim for me, an insurance plan that was fairly new then. The claim's adjustor told me a day or two later that I would receive $8 a week to compensate for the time I could not work. I tried to explain to him that I only earned $1.50 a week and only worked a day a week, but was told that $8 was the minimum benefit. In the end, I received $40 total, which allowed me to buy a new suit, shoes, a shirt, and a tie for my high school graduation.

Marshall, which had a population of 4,590 in 1940, then had two or three grocery stores, a couple of men's clothing stores, a furniture store, and two or three hardware stores, banks, and jewelry stores. As the county seat, we also had the courthouse and jail.

My graduation suit paid for with $40 in worker's compensation claim. I tried to explain that I didn't earn that much money, but the $40 was the minimum payment over five weeks that I missed work. Unfortunately, you can't see my shoes.

Of the 100 students in my graduating class of 1939, maybe ten or twelve—mostly the sons of doctors, lawyers, and bankers—could afford to go straight to college after high school. Most graduates simply could not afford it. I took a job as a bellhop at the New Atlantic Hotel in Marshall, where my hours were split: 7 a.m. to 9:30 a.m., 11:30 a.m. to 1:30 p.m., and 4 to 10 p.m. I did not wear a uniform like you see in movies; it was not that sophisticated a hotel.

I was happy to have a job that paid me $5 a week plus tips. Mostly, I received dimes from guests for carrying their bags up to rooms and back down for checkout. I had one wife-cheating doctor as a customer from a neighboring town who made a monthly "sick call" on a woman who came to Marshall from Minneapolis. This doctor arrived with his medical bag for this exam, leaving sometime during the night. She gave me a 75-cent or occasionally dollar tip when she checked out, healthy again.

Another good customer was the field director for the Caterpillar Tractor Company. A former offensive lineman for the Chicago Bears from 1931 to 1932 and for the Cincinnati Reds in 1933, he was a giant for his era at 6'4" and 248 pounds. Lloyd Burdick came through Marshall every six to eight weeks, staying for a couple nights when he called on implement dealers in Northern Iowa and Minnesota. He was interested in my Uncle Pete in the Green Bay Packers and became a very good friend who occasionally gave me a dollar tip.

During some of my time off, I took naps in Dr. Jacquot's

offices, which were on the first floor of the hotel. Beginning in high school, I lived with Aunt Ollie and Grandmother Regnier in town, since there was no school bus in those days from the farm into town. I helped them with home and yard chores like I would do if I had still been on the farm: lawn work, shoveling snow, and keeping the furnace going in winter. My sister Betty was there with me for awhile as well. She helped out in the kitchen and with some of the housework.

The opportunity to live with Grandma and Aunt Ollie passed to other kids in our family and was good for everyone involved. It helped my grandmother and aunt, and it meant I could save every dollar I earned as a bellhop and later when I went back to Economy as a full-time employee.

Eventually, I had enough money to go to the Minnesota School of Business, one of two then in Minneapolis and one in St. Paul that offered one-year courses to prepare men and women for business jobs. The school is now known outside of the state of Minnesota as Globe University.

I thought I had enough money to last through that entire course, which I began in March 1941, but I found myself in dire straits three weeks before completion. I had some part-time jobs while I was in school there, including correcting student papers for the head of the Accounting Department for 40 cents an hour. If I went home for a long weekend, I picked up some money working at Olson & Lowe Clothiers, whose owner was the father of one of my classmates. This was a very classy store, where you dressed in suit and tie to serve customers.

I nursed my savings as well as I could, but it came down to the wire. I spoke with the school about moving to the evening program, which would take me a bit longer but could be completed while I worked—assuming I found a job quickly. A day or so after I visited the Placement Office at the school seeking help, the school sent me out on an interview with General Mills, which was and is headquartered in Minneapolis. After several interviews, I was thrilled to be hired as a junior accountant in the McKnight Building, where I began on October 23, 1941, just three days after I left day school. This was my first career-track employment, and I was earning $80 a month, good starting wages in those days for college graduates, let alone my shorter program that I had not quite finished. General Mills recognized I would finish via night school, which I did. This job came just in time. When I received my first paycheck from General Mills, I was down to 40 cents in savings and a couple streetcar tokens. I cut it that close.

CHAPTER TWO

Fighting the Depression and Preparing for War

With instantaneous broadcasts 24 hours a day today, it is hard to imagine just how advanced radio seemed in the 1930s and 1940s as a technology—until the batteries died and we couldn't hear our favorite show. The main battery, about the size of a car battery today, could be recharged in town, while the other batteries had to be replaced.

Before we had our own, we went to our neighbor's to listen to radio programs on an Atwater Kent radio, which had multiple dials that were tuned to hear a broadcast. I remember the fight between Jack Dempsey and Gene Tunney in 1927, where supposedly the count on the downed Tunney went to 14 instead of the usual 10. Tunney came back and eventually won on points, causing a controversy in the boxing world. We also heard the fights between Joe Louis and the German Max Schmeling in 1936 and 1938, battles that were considered to be proxies for actual war between the Untied States and Germany. Schmeling won the first, but Louis came back in 1938 to knock out Schmeling in 124 seconds. Across America, we were thrilled.

Boxers and boxing were as popular as the National Football League is today. After business college, my brother Jim went to work for the Hamm Brewing Company in St. Paul, Minnesota. Jim got to know some of the boxers whom his boss managed. It was a thrill for us kids when Jim brought home some of these fighters, including Marv Wason, whom we read about in boxing newspapers like *The Ring*. Wason, who had some early success, later was beaten often enough to have a permanently flattened nose. When he came home with Jim one time, he encouraged us boys to take up boxing. It was a big deal to have a boxer we had read about in our home.

A big baseball fan, my father enjoyed listening to baseball games broadcast on the radio. When my youngest brother was born on the opening day of the World Series in 1934, he was named Dean after Dizzy Dean, who had a 30–7 regular season pitching record that year for the Cardinals. His brother Paul was also successful as a pitcher for the Cardinals that year, earning a 19–6 record that season. My mother joked it was a good thing that the pitcher that day did not have a long name that would be difficult to spell and pronounce.

Listening to War News

Radio had some shows for kids like "Jack Armstrong, All American Boy," and broadcasted some major sporting events like the Chicago Blackhawks hockey games and baseball's World Series. We listened intently to the news broadcasts of men like Edward R. Murrow and William Shirer on our Atwater Kent radio. I also remember President Franklin Roosevelt's Fireside

Chats on Saturday nights. We felt hope for the future when he described steps being taken to improve the economy.

During his first 100 days in office in 1933, Congress enacted an amazing number of laws geared to combat unemployment of 25 percent to 30 percent. As the aide to U.S. Rep. Magnus Johnson in Congress, Uncle Chick had a front row seat to the history made that year. Among the many acts passed was the Civilian Conservation Corps (CCC), which was part of the Works Progress Administration (WPA). They put young men to work on a variety of projects for the good of the country. Other programs in the WPA put men to work in jobs that met the country's needs for bridges, buildings, and other public services, including arts projects. These jobs were a big boost to our economy, as paid work meant they had money to spend in their communities and actually paid taxes back to the government. These were vitally important programs for our country as a whole and individuals within it.

Among those benefiting from the CCC was my future brother-in-law, Hugh Thompson, who never gave a thought about the cost of continuing his education until his father lost the small-town bank he owned during the Depression. Hugh, who had gone to River Falls State College in Wisconsin, had planned on medical school. But his family had joined so many others in very tough economic circumstances. If he wanted to medical school, he had to find a way to go himself.

Roosevelt's Tree Army, as some called the CCC, provided young unmarried men with work in a service run by the Army. These men were provided room, board, and work clothes plus $25 a month for backbreaking work, with all but $5 sent home to the family or into a bank as savings. After the first year, Hugh got a $5-a-month raise.

For the rest of his life, Hugh—my sister Betty's husband—said the CCC made it possible for him to attend medical school and have a wonderful career. He met Betts at Asbury Hospital in Minneapolis, where she was a registered nurse and he an intern.

Betts joined Hugh in California, where they were married, after he found her a job as a surgical nurse at San Bernardino County Hospital where he was in a surgical residency. He did not finish the residency because he was drafted after Pearl Harbor. Betts then took a job in Seattle, where the troopship Hugh staffed as a medical officer returned—infrequently—after voyages delivering soldiers to various assignments in the Pacific.

As difficult as it was to get by during the Depression, we also worried about events in Europe, particularly whether we might be drawn into another world war. It was chilling to hear radio broadcasts from Europe in the late 1930s about what was happening in the countries that later would be called the Axis (Japan, Italy, Germany, and Russia—until the Nazis turned around and attacked it; that's when Russia joined our side).

Historians trace the seeds leading to World War II to the end of World War I, when Germany was forced to sign the Versailles Treaty that severely punished that country economically. People were susceptible to a person like Adolf Hitler, who prom-

My brother-in-law Hugh Thompson said he would not have gone to medical school if he had not been in the Civilian Conservation Corps during the Great Depression. He is shown here on the left with Dick, my brother, on the right.

ised them a new order. He became the leader of the National Socialist Party (Nazi) in 1921 and published *Mein Kampf* in 1925, which told of his plans for the future of Germany. Hitler became part of the German government as chancellor in 1933, and then after the German President Paul von Hindenburg died, Hitler became "Fuehrer and Reich Chancellor" in 1935, giving him complete dictatorship.

Hitler then began taking over territories that would benefit Germany—and his personal power—beginning with Austria in March 1938. He collected other countries without much effort, including the Sudetenland, the Czech lands, and then Poland in 1939 with the help of Russia. Within the next two years, Germany invaded Denmark and Norway, followed by Luxemburg, the Netherlands, Belgium, and France.

Russia, which had signed a pact with Germany, took the Eastern side of Poland in 1939, while Germany occupied the Western portion. Later, Germany attacked Russia, something that actually improved the Allied chances for victory since it split the German forces to have two theaters of war. Japan, meanwhile, had invaded Manchuria and China in 1931 and 1936, respectively. Italy attacked Ethiopia in 1935 and Albania in 1939.

In my last year of high school, we all wondered when and how the United States would enter the war. Most of our political leaders were isolationists, preferring to stay out of what they did not consider a U.S. problem. World events—most specifically the Japanese attack on Pearl Harbor on December 7, 1941—forced the United States into the war.

Thankfully, President Roosevelt had the foresight to know that ultimately we could not avoid war despite the desire of isolationists. He convinced Congress to pass the Selective Service Act in 1940, which required men from ages 21 to 35 to register for potential military training. Later, the age dropped to 18 when more men were needed.

Once we reached the age when we could be drafted, Selective Service Boards called men for service for what originally was to be just 12 months. Many had not completed their year of service when war was declared. They were then in the military for the duration. I was not 21 when the law passed so I did not have to register immediately.

What I liked about the law was its fairness. We all had the same chance of being called to duty through our local board's lottery system. During World War II, people of all economic levels served together.

Since the end of Vietnam, we've had a voluntary military, which sounds good on the surface, except in practice it is not always fair. The poor and minorities are more highly represented in the military, because many believe the service gives them better economic opportunities to make a living and better prepare for careers after the military.

Pearl Harbor

On December 7, 1941, I was at my Uncle Chick's house, getting a much-appreciated home-cooked meal. I enjoyed being with family so much that I volunteered to do odd jobs around his house, such as painting their basement. By this time, Uncle Chick had left his political career and instead had a state civil service job.

That afternoon, we heard the "news flash" on the radio that the Japanese had bombed the U.S. Naval Base at Pearl Harbor, Hawaii, at 7:48 a.m. Hawaiian time or about 1:48 p.m. Central

THIRD WAR EXTRA

MUCH COLDER

Minneapolis Morning Tribune

FOUNDED IN 1867

MINNEAPOLIS, MINN., MONDAY, DECEMBER 8, 1941 — Price 3 Cents

JAPS OPEN WAR ON U. S.!

Hawaii and Guam Attacked; Wake Island Seized; Casualties Run High; Oklahoma Set Fire

BULLETINS

'LICK HELL OUT OF THEM'—WHEELER

BILLINGS, MONT.—(AP)—"The only thing now is to do our best to lick hell out of them," Senator Burton K. Wheeler of Montana said Sunday after learning of the Japanese attack on Hawaii and the Philippines. Wheeler has been a leading spokesman against intervention in the European war.

Sen. Gerald P. Nye, (R., N. D., said at Pittsburgh, the attack was "just what Britain had planned for us." "Britain has been getting this ready since 1938," he said.

San Pedro Posts Guard

Here's Your Time Table for Pacific

U. S. Planes in Air

NIPPON PLANE CARRIER, 4 SUBS REPORTED SUNK

By THE ASSOCIATED PRESS

War between the United States and Japan exploded violently in the Pacific Sunday as waves of Japanese bombers twice attacked Honolulu, inflicting apparently great loss in life and property, and bombed the [illegible] U. S. base at Guam, midway between Hawaii and the Philippines.

A Reuters (British news agency) dispatch from Shanghai quoted unconfirmed reports saying the Japanese had occupied U. S.-owned Wake island, between Guam and Hawaii.

A Japanese aircraft carrier was sunk off Honolulu Sunday, according to United Press reporting a broadcast by the Panama radio heard in New York.

NBC reports from Honolulu said 350 men had been killed by a direct bomb hit on Hickman field and that the U. S. battleship Oklahoma had been set afire in Pearl harbor.

The war department's first official estimate of deaths was much lower, however. Army chiefs told the White House there were 104 known dead and more than 300 wounded in the army forces. These figures did not include civilian casualties.

Two other U. S. warships also were reported attacked in the harbor.

Army officials said at least two Japanese planes had been shot down in the Honolulu area, where the death toll was listed at seven, including three whites, two Japanese and a [illegible]-year-old Portuguese girl.

U. S. CLAIMS 4 SUBMARINES

THE PACIFIC FRONTIER

U.S.S.R. — ALASKA — MONGOLIA — CHINA — JAPAN — DUTCH EAST INDIES — AUSTRALIA

PACIFIC BASES — UNITED STATES — OTHER POWERS

Canada's Cabinet Called — 'Frisco Mobilizes — Borders Closed to Japs — Panama Arresting All Jap Nationals — FBI Ready for Jap Espionage — Canada Calls Fliers — Japs Burn Documents — Alaska Calls Banned — Hongkong Volunteers

BLACK-OUT IN CANAL ZONE

CHURCHILL SUMMONS PARLIAMENT

150 PLANES IN INITIAL ASSAULT

BOMBARDED BY WARSHIP

I saved this Extra edition after the Pearl Harbor bombing.

time. The news instantly sobered us, and I'm not talking about alcohol but recognition of how dramatically life changed. I took the streetcar home, wanting to get back to my rooming house before dark. No one said much on that ride; we were all lost in our thoughts about what was to come.

The next morning, I picked up copies of newspapers that I have kept all these years. Large, bold headlines proclaimed the treachery of the Japanese attack. The mood was dour at the lunch counter in the McKnight Building, where I usually took my breakfast before starting work at General Mills. All the young men talked about what was probably ahead for us; we all expected to enter the service.

President Franklin D. Roosevelt described the surprise attack as "a day that will live in infamy." It was shocking because we learned that U.S. officials were negotiating with the Japanese Ambassador in Washington, D.C., at the time of the bombing. Japan attacked the U.S. to prevent our Navy and Air Corps from supporting Great Britain and other countries. Japan also was interested in conquering more lands, especially in Southeast Asia.

Newspapers described how the surprise Japanese attack devastated our Navy, sinking or damaging three cruisers, three destroyers, an anti-aircraft training ship, and a minelayer. Also, the Japanese destroyed 188 U.S. planes that were on the ground at the time of the attack. All told, some 2,402 Americans were killed and 1,282 were wounded. The U.S. declared war on Japan on December 8, 1941, and Germany and Italy joined Japan in declaring war on the United States.

Many young men rushed to get into the fight after Pearl Harbor, but I was in no hurry, as I finally had employment with career potential and jobs were scarce then. I figured—correctly—that I would be called for duty eventually.

I registered with the Hennepin County Selective Service Board in Minneapolis and was called in for a physical exam to determine whether I was physically capable of being a soldier. I had my 21st birthday on October 15, 1942, and received notice the next day that I was classified 1A, which meant I was available immediately for the draft. My roommate, Ralph Freed, already was in the Army.

I was ordered for induction on December 15, 1942, at the Armory in Minneapolis, where I joined many other men who had gotten their draft orders. After being sworn in, we went on furlough until the day after Christmas, when we were to report back to the Armory.

It was wonderful to have that last holiday at home with my family, but I said good-bye to my family on Christmas Day to make sure I arrived at the armory in Minneapolis at the appointed time. Mother was emotional; she had already said good-bye to Bill a year or two before me. My dad had tears in his eyes when I left, something I had never seen before. We were not a warrior family, but we realized that World War II was a necessary war and that we must all do our part. Brother Jim was disqualified because of a heart murmur. My brother Wally would be called into the Army once he graduated high

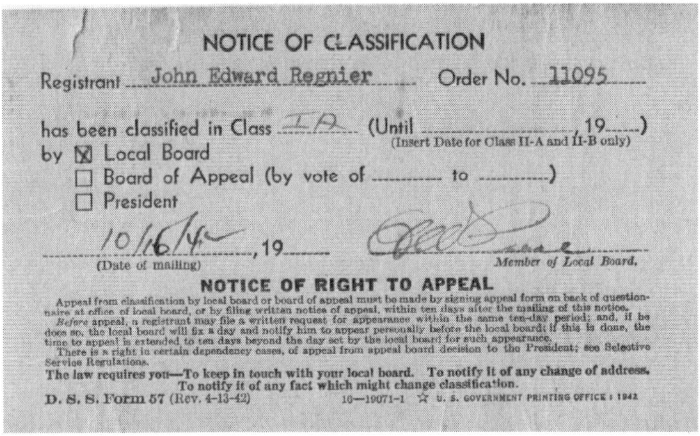

NOTICE OF CLASSIFICATION

Registrant John Edward Regnier Order No. 11095

has been classified in Class I A (Until ...., 19.....)
(Insert Date for Class II-A and II-B only)
by ☒ Local Board
☐ Board of Appeal (by vote of .... to ....)
☐ President

10/16/42, 19......
(Date of mailing)

Member of Local Board.

NOTICE OF RIGHT TO APPEAL

Appeal from classification by local board or board of appeal must be made by signing appeal form on back of questionnaire at office of local board, or by filing written notice of appeal, within ten days after the mailing of this notice.

Before appeal, a registrant may file a written request for appearance within the same ten-day period; and, if he does so, the local board will fix a day and notify him to appear personally before the local board; if this is done, the time to appeal is extended to ten days beyond the day set by the local board for such appearance.

There is a right in certain dependency cases, of appeal from appeal board decision to the President; see Selective Service Regulations.

The law requires you—To keep in touch with your local board. To notify it of any change of address. To notify it of any fact which might change classification.

D. S. S. Form 57 (Rev. 4-13-42) 16—19071-1 ☆ U. S. GOVERNMENT PRINTING OFFICE : 1942

My 1-A card arrived the day after my 21st birthday. It made me immediately available for military service.

school and had turned 18—the draft age by then.

After reporting to the armory on December 26, 1942, the Army immediately transported us to Fort Snelling. Some 300,000 men and women joined the Armed Forces during World War II from Fort Snelling, which handled up to 800 recruits a day during its peak in 1942. Located at the confluence of the Minnesota River and Mississippi River in Hennepin County, the fort is now operated by the Minnesota Historical Society as Historic Fort Snelling.

I knew no one that day I was processed until I ran into a friend who had worked in the accounting department at General Mills. Herman Sogard was a second lieutenant assigned to the medical administration corps. It was nice to see a familiar face, because everything was so overwhelming as we moved in our boxer shorts from doctor to doctor who gave us a complete physical, including eyes, ears, nose, throat, chest, legs, and feet.

That same day, an officer provided a broad orientation to the Army, including such issues as our outward appearance as servicemen (clean and correctly arranged uniform, properly worn and adjusted equipment, and manner of behavior in and out of formation). We already saluted officers and answered, "Yes, sir" and "No, sir," when they spoke to us. We knew we would learn much more through basic training, including the importance of developing unit cohesion and following orders as a group. They also showed us movies warning us about venereal disease.

After being assigned to barracks, I was given my first Army responsibility—latrine duty. I had to get the 20 toilets and urinals ready for inspection. When an officer and others following him inspected my latrine, I was told I had missed a spot on one of the toilets. I took care of it right after he left—and, happily, latrine duty lasted only one day.

The next day we had a full day of testing that we were told was very important to our future in the Army. It was an easy decision for me to stay in the barracks rather than getting a pass as many of the men did for a night on the town. I wanted to concentrate and not be overly tired for the testing, which included the Army General Classification Test (AGCT), a battery that included intelligence, interest, and aptitude. I had a sense that how I did on that exam might be important for future assignments in the Army after basic training.

At the end of my Fort Snelling processing, I was given orders and train tickets to Camp McLain outside of Grenada, Mississippi, where I was assigned to a newly-formed medical regiment for basic training. Assignments were based on the rapidly-expanding Army's need to build regiments after Pearl Harbor. You never knew in advance what type of unit you would be assigned to until you completed your induction center processing. Testing results were more important after basic training, not for the initial training. My roommate, Ralph Freed, who went in three or four months before me, was sent to an armored infantry division in Camp Campbell, Kentucky.

Basic Training

My train ticket allowed me to stop for a few hours to see my younger sister, Irene, known in our family as Tiny, who was living in Chicago. After our short visit, I got on a train to Mississippi, arriving at night at Camp McCain. It was foreign territory to me, not at all what I expected. But then I had little experience beyond Minnesota.

Camp McCain, which now is a Mississippi National Guard Training Center, trained about 50,000 troops during its peak in World War II. I didn't know it at the time, but the camp also housed about 7,800 German prisoners of war.

The newly-formed 331st Medical Regiment consisted of 1,200 men mostly coming from places in the Midwest, including Minnesota, Iowa, and North and South Dakota. We had a large group from New York and New Jersey and a few recruits from southern states like Texas and Oklahoma. We were mostly in our 20s, although we had a few older men of 30 to 35. None of us knew what was ahead of us.

One surprise was the temperature; I assumed it would be warmer in the South, even in January. It was a damp cold at night, and we were miserable, not the way I pictured the South. Our barrack's heat source came from two little potbellied stoves. But first we had to figure out how to start the fires in them. Some impatient guys from New Jersey tried to fill the stove with coal found outside and then throw matches at it. They swore profusely when it did not light.

After we Midwesterners got our stove going with a bit of paper as kindling, these New Jersey guys snuck down to get warm. They told us we had an advantage in knowing how to use the heaters. I shook my head and responded, "Your problem is that you just stand and swear at each other and throw matches at the stove. You don't take the time to figure out how to start a fire. We've never seen this kind of stove before either."

Basic training began each morning with an hour of calisthenics before breakfast. I was in pretty good shape and young, so the workout was not so difficult for me. I think the values I learned growing up during the Depression also helped. I was used to hard physical work and not expecting anything to be just handed to me. I also learned to be creative on the farm, where we didn't have the luxury to get new things all the time.

We learned to be resourceful.

Basic training included many hikes in full packs and drills, including an obstacle course in which we had to crawl under barbed wire 18 inches above ground at night while blanks were fired over us. At one point we came to a wall that required us to jump into a sandpit. I landed heavily on my right foot, which led me to go on sick call the next day. It took most of the day to be seen by a general doctor who then referred me to a podiatrist. He taped my foot and prescribed a Thomas heel, which modified my shoe until my sprained ankle healed.

I did get excused from marching for a few days and part of the last 10-mile march in full pack near the end of that basic training. My foot got better, but as the doctor predicted back in 1943, I have had more problems with it as I've aged.

I considered basic training to be rigorous but good for us. Of course, along with it came duties—such as kitchen duty (KP), which was a terrible experience. You worked under the constant hollering of the mess sergeant who ordered to you set up tables, bring in food, fix huge tubs of vegetables, and then do cleanup. We served a lot of mutton, which was so bad that most was tossed into the garbage.

A few of the men in our barracks had no consideration for those of us who were exhausted and ready to hit the sack at night. Instead of being quiet, they were loud and crude, keeping us from much-needed sleep. Three of them, who were right across from my bunk, were especially obnoxious late into the evening.

It was at Fort McCain that I met my friend, Fred Kercheval, with whom I shared that camera in 1945. Both promoted to sergeant during that first year in the Army, we stayed together for the rest of the war except for our last few months of occupation in Germany after the war ended in Europe. We forged such a strong bond that our friendship continued lifelong between our two families.

Assigned to a Supply Unit off a Garbage Truck

Despite that testing back at Fort Snelling that was supposed to help determine future assignments in the Army, I ended up with my job assignment by chance. During basic training, you have many more duties beyond military drills. They included the much disliked KP and garbage collecting. We also did all sorts of work related to building the new camp, including constructing sidewalks.

One day I was on garbage truck duty with five or six other men picking up trash from around the camp. When we stopped to pick up garbage at the supply building, a sergeant came out and asked if any of us could type. I hesitated before responding, having been told that it might be a mistake to volunteer too quickly for anything in the Army. But still, a job typing sounded good to me from the vantage point of that garbage truck.

After I told that sergeant that I learned typing in business school, he invited me into his office in the supply department. This sergeant clearly did not care a bit about whether I had good scores on those placement exams. The only score that mattered to him was how fast I could type, which would help his department. I typed a bunch of reports, which apparently were good enough for the sergeant to want me in his unit. He told me, however, that I would have to finish basic training first. Until then, I typed part-time in the supply department when I was not training. It got me out of KP and garbage duty.

I'm proud to say I was recruited off the garbage truck.

Furlough after Basic Training

After I finished basic, I had a week's furlough, which I took in St. Paul, where I planned to stay with my Uncle Hank and Aunt Marceline before going to Marshall to see my parents. After I got off the train at St. Paul, I stood waiting for a streetcar to take me to Uncle Hank's home in West St. Paul. Before the streetcar arrived, a car pulled up and the man in back asked where I was going and if I needed a ride.

It turned out to be Minnesota Governor Edward John Thye, who served from April 27, 1943, to January 8, 1947. He had taken over after Governor Harold Stassen joined the Navy. When I introduced myself to Governor Thye, he asked if I was related to Henry Regnier. When I confirmed I was his nephew and that I was actually going to his house, he said his wife was in a women's group with my Aunt Marc. I found the governor to be down to earth, a nice guy who had once been a farmer in southern Minnesota prior to entering politics. Wearing a uniform made getting rides easy during the war, although not so many from a governor.

Sgt. Fred Kercheval became a lifelong friend of mine.

Here I am at Camp Forrest in Tennessee.

182nd Medical Battalion

After basic training, the regiment was split into two battalions, the 181st and the 182nd. I was assigned to be the supply sergeant for the 182nd Medical Battalion Headquarters Unit. We were then transferred to Camp Forrest, Tennessee, near Tullahoma, a town of 4,000 that grew to 75,000 by the war's end because of the military buildup. Forrest was a big improvement over McCain.

Forrest had been a National Guard Training camp named after Tennessee Governor Austin Peay until it was rebuilt beginning in 1940 and renamed for Confederate General Nathan Bedford Forrest. Ultimately, the camp grew to be 85,000 acres.[7]

Located 70 miles south of Nashville, Camp Forrest trained infantry, artillery, signal organization, and cooks. It also served as a hospital center and temporary encampment for troops doing maneuvers. Among those who brought his men to Camp Forrest for training was then Major General George Patton.

We left Forrest for Army maneuvers during the spring and summer of 1943 in the hills of Tennessee. While these large infantry units fought in mock warfare events, we set up supply tents and first aid stations as part of our medical battalion's work. We responded to some injuries during the war games, but none life-threatening. One soldier lost a finger after his wedding ring caught on a metal strip on a truck as he jumped out. Bleeding profusely, the man was taken to our field hospital, where a doctor amputated the soldier's finger right there in the tent facility—as the doctor would do at a field hospital overseas.

A photo at this time shows us in our tent city, where we lived for a good part of the summer of 1944. The picture shows me washing my uniform in a bucket with a helmet full of water and a bar of soap. We dried our laundry in trees.

I was not aware at the time that Camp Forrest also served another purpose during the war, as a detention camp for aliens that the United States rounded up after Pearl Harbor under the Alien Enemy Control Program. With so many arrested and held without charges, the Justice Department used military camps to house the prisoners.

Beginning in May 1942, Camp Forrest became an internment camp for on average 200 men, mostly Italians, until 600 German prisoners arrived in November 1942. The peak population was more than 800.[8] Internees were later transferred to other locations when Forrest became a prisoner-of-war camp.

We had no knowledge of or any contact with prisoners; instead we spent our time on playing war, doing maneuvers designed to prepare us for the war overseas. Our headquarters battalion consisted of four to six companies responsible for what was first called "clearing and collecting" but later ambulance companies.

Culture Shock

Before I had gotten my induction notice, I visited a friend who was in the Army at a camp near Little Rock, Arkansas. It was the first time my friend and I had been out of Minnesota and

Here I am doing my laundry on maneuvers in Tennessee.

certainly the first time we had seen segregation, but it was nothing compared to what we witnessed in Mississippi.

The South was a cultural shock for most of us from the North because of the overt racism. History books say Abraham Lincoln freed the slaves with the Emancipation Proclamation during the Civil War, but that didn't seem to be the case in Mississippi, Alabama, and other places in the South. The military was still segregated until after the war when President Harry Truman ordered integration of the armed services through Executive Order 9981 on July 25, 1948, abolishing racial discrimination in the armed services.

One of the men in my unit from Texas took great pride in talking about the number of blacks who worked for his family cooking, cleaning, and caring for their children. But he would not ride in a car or go to school with them. I had no desire to spend much time with him. When we went into the small town near this camp north of Jackson, Mississippi, I saw signs on water fountains that said, "Whites only" and "Colored only." It made me sick. These soldiers also told sick jokes about all sorts of ethnic groups, which made me uncomfortable.

After our maneuvers, Fred and I got weekend passes to see my high school friends, Ed and Elizabeth Marks, who were in Huntsville, Alabama, where Ed was stationed with the ordinance corps. We picked up our bus tickets at the PX—Post Exchange—a kind of convenience store on the base. When the Jefferson Lines bus pulled up, we were puzzled to see so many men standing in the aisle of the bus when there were empty seats in the back.

The idea of standing for hours to Huntsville was not appealing so we pushed our way to the back through the men standing in the aisle. These men glared at us so much that Fred and I felt if we hadn't been in uniform, we would have been goners. We got to the back and sat on the platform seat, where there were several empty seats between a black soldier and a black woman.

Avoiding eye contact, this soldier said, "You guys must be

from the North." He told me that this section of the bus was for "colored people." Neither Fred nor I had noticed the sign above the section. We just wanted to sit down.

I was curious about this soldier so we started talking. He told me he had been selected to go to a black medical college in Nashville to become a doctor for black soldiers. Clearly, he was far more intelligent than some of the civilian men who glared at us for hours while standing in the aisle. The soldier also told me he hoped the bus driver would stop a couple miles before town at a gas station where his family planned to pick him up. The occasion was his completing the first five months of medical school.

The driver pulled up to the station just as the soldier had requested. A wonderful group of family and friends who clearly loved him greeted him. I could see he had much more to offer than that prejudiced group standing in the aisle of the bus.

I had heard a bit about Jim Crow Laws that separated blacks from whites. But the overt racism was almost as shocking to me as seeing combat injuries later.

That was not the only prejudice I encountered in the Army. After one of the guys in my unit went to a Baptist church, one of the women suggested he bring a friend to a church picnic that afternoon. I went with him and visited with a young lady who was quite active in the church. In our conversation, she said one thing she could never do was date a Catholic. I listened to her for awhile and pumped her a bit about her feelings. Once I had her far enough out on a limb, I told her that I was about to say something shocking to her.

"I'm Catholic," I told her.

She spent the rest of the picnic trying to apologize for what she had said to me. This was the first and last time I saw her, but I hope she learned that as a Catholic, I'm not that much different from the other guys.

One of the guys in our unit shared that view of Catholics, spewing hate about Republicans, Catholics, dogs, and the N-word. I witnessed even more absolutely foolish and dangerous prejudice in Europe.

Alerted for Going Overseas

Shortly after we finished maneuvers, I was told I was being considered for officer's training school. Before I could go through the interview process, our battalion was "frozen" in anticipation for being sent overseas. This meant no one could leave us or transfer into our unit, except for a medical reason.

We did not know where we were going, but a friend from basic training gave me a very strong hint that proved to be accurate. During basic, a call went out to all units seeking high-speed typists, who could test for positions on the clerical staff in Army Headquarters in Washington, D.C. A Fuller Brush salesman before the war, Herb Woods was chosen for this work because he could type 70 words per minute on the old standard typewriter. I could type, but nothing like he could, a reason he was assigned to work for several high-ranking officers at the predecessor for the Pentagon.

Herb wrote me a letter from the Defense Department that began with this plea: "Please burn this letter after reading." He told me he had been filing in a drawer marked "secret" when he unexpectedly found our unit's orders to Europe. This man was always a loose cannon. While he was authorized to be in that drawer because of his work, sharing what he found was very risky for him. I kept his secret and told no one. When we received our orders, I was less surprised than the rest of our unit about where we were going. I preferred assignment to Europe because at least we would go to developed countries instead of the jungles of the Pacific theater.

With our departure from Forrest, I took out a diary that a relative gave me when I went into the Army. I didn't write every day—often there was no time—but the diary and letters support my memories and provide my voice from the time of events. I begin with the entry that referred to the start of our journey overseas. You will notice that at times I just wrote partial sentences because of how busy we were.

31 July 1944

Departed Camp Forrest, Tennessee en route to Camp Shanks, New York at 2100. (Pullmans, Chow, Dirt, etc.) Chattanooga, Atlanta, Washington DC, Newark, New York.

From Forrest, we took a troop train to Camp Shanks in New York, about 15 miles outside of New York City. This camp was dubbed "Last Stop, USA" because it was the largest point of embarkation for soldiers headed for the front lines in North

Africa and Europe during World War II, including those landing on D-Day at Normandy.[9]

According to the online Camp Shanks Museum, the camp consisted of 1,500 barracks, mess halls, theaters, a hospital, and other buildings. About 1.5 million GIs (roughly 40,000 a month) were issued combat equipment and underwent final inspections before shipping overseas. Most soldiers spent eight to twelve days there. While at Shanks, we had additional training in abandoning ship and using a gas mask, reminders of how real it was to go into a war zone.

We also were given passes on two occasions that allowed us to see New York City, a new experience for this small-town boy. Other soldiers hit the taverns, but we decided to go to fancy restaurants and see plays on Broadway. As a soldier we usually had opportunities for less expensive tickets.

7 August 1944

First pass to NY City on 5 Aug. Went with Schaefer, Gonzales, Amsler, and Kercheval. Bars, Empire State (picture) Radio City, French Café, unable to read menus, (Gonny) Back up town, Stage Play "Catherine Was Great" w/ Mae West. Hotel Astor, Waldorf Astoria, spent most of evening at Glass Hat nightclub—very good. Riding subways, eating, etc.

Second pass to NY City on 7 Aug. Went with Schaefer, Gonzales, and Amsler. Arrived early, walked around heart of city. Ate with Miller, Eden, Campbell, etc. Went to Stage Play "One Touch of Venus" w/ Mary Martin and John Boles,

Schubert Theatre. Very good. Went to Stage Door Canteen, disappointed.

While we were at Camp Shanks, we saw other entertainment, including a boxing card with James J. Braddock, who was World Heavyweight Champion from 1935 to 1937. Braddock was older when we saw him, but was trying to work his way back into competition for another chance at the title. We also attended USO shows, which entertained us with well-known performers.

Then the day came that we were ordered to the ship. As I wrote in my diary on August 8, 1944, "Turned in khakis and rolled pack for the last time, sweating it out."

A train took us into the Port of New York, from which we marched in full gear on our backs to the SS John Ericsson, a ship originally called the SS Kungsholm. The U.S. purchased the Kungsholm in 1941 from the Swedish American Line (SAL), renamed it, and modified as a troopship. After the war, SAL bought the ship back in 1947.

10 August 1944

Marched to train, very hot, packs heavy, train dirty, crowded, morale getting lower. Long march from train to ferry. Nearly dead when I got on ferry, but revived when started breathing fresh air. Ferry across Hudson River. Long march from ferry to docks, Red Cross women w/ lemonade. Down the pier and up the gang plank, funny feeling. Boarded SS John Erickson at 2300, remained in Port until following

> day. E Deck, very crowded, hot, terrible odor. Stacked 5 high, sweat ran through all the nests (Kerch, me, Eden, and Dog). Morale low, everyone miserable and bitching. No air, couldn't leave hole, soaked in soot and dirt and couldn't get clean in salt water. Over 6,000 troops aboard. Next morning got to go up on deck, most wonderful feeling in the world to get fresh air. Went to chow, had to leave before finishing. Went back on deck all morning. Departed Staten Island Port of Embarkation at 1330, wasn't sure where we were going but rumors were Liverpool, England.

This was a depressing night as it was miserably warm and we were in our fall and winter uniforms since we were heading to Europe. The train itself was stifling hot and the windows did not open. We were so desperate for air that we wanted to kick out the windows. After we arrived at the port, we marched quite a distance from the train depot in full pack.

On ship, we each were handed a Bible and a letter from President Roosevelt.

Once on board, we marched down five or six levels to our assigned quarters in the bowels of the ship. Five bunks were stacked on top of each other with little space between them. We knew the oldest guy in our unit, Sgt. Art Eden, would never make it up to his assigned third tier bunk, so one of us shoved him into a lower bunk and took his. With so little air exchange, these hot quarters were oppressively overwhelming. Hundreds and hundreds of us—between 7,000 and 8,000—were in the same boat, literally and figuratively. The only opportunity to wash was with

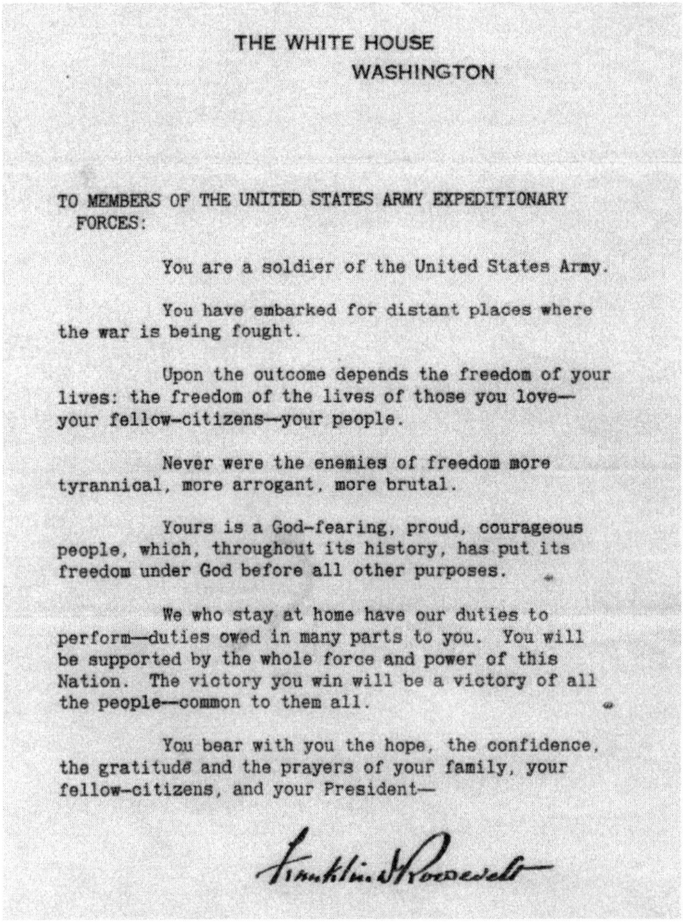

THE WHITE HOUSE
WASHINGTON

TO MEMBERS OF THE UNITED STATES ARMY EXPEDITIONARY FORCES:

You are a soldier of the United States Army.

You have embarked for distant places where the war is being fought.

Upon the outcome depends the freedom of your lives: the freedom of the lives of those you love—your fellow-citizens—your people.

Never were the enemies of freedom more tyrannical, more arrogant, more brutal.

Yours is a God-fearing, proud, courageous people, which, throughout its history, has put its freedom under God before all other purposes.

We who stay at home have our duties to perform—duties owed in many parts to you. You will be supported by the whole force and power of this Nation. The victory you win will be a victory of all the people—common to them all.

You bear with you the hope, the confidence, the gratitude and the prayers of your family, your fellow-citizens, and your President—

Franklin D Roosevelt

President Roosevelt's letter to soldiers in the U.S. Army Expeditionary Force.

seawater, and you couldn't lather with salt water.

It looked like we were in for a very long, miserable crossing because so many of us were crammed into such a small space, but then we caught a break. As one of our on-board projects, we were assigned to the ship's medical unit to provide extra help, particularly in administering two immunizations to each man before we landed. Fred and I were put to work giving shots after an hour of training. We used the same syringe over and over, although we put in a newly-sterilized needle each time. Men lined up in a big open area, and we worked many hours on each of two days. These shots went well unless the needles had a curve or bend to them.

11 August to 22 August 1944

At sea. Very lucky first day, entire Detachment [battalion headquarters group] assigned to work in Ships Hosp. Fred, Underwood, Rudy, and I in Medical Ward. Col. Sandy and Maj. Cicero is charge. Ate 3 meals a day in Permanent Staff Mess hall, good food. Capt, Kramer, 1st Sgt. Dolon, Frank Cole, "Animal Trainer," etc. Hosp. Work interesting. Gave shots to 6000 men twice. Attended Mass regularly. Pretty rough sleeping in the hole, odor getting worse every day. Slept out on deck 2 nights, wonderful. Last 2 nights slept in ward. Found out we were going to Liverpool about 5th day at sea. Picked up our convoy 2nd day out, 68 ships, as far as one could see. Destroyer Escorts for protection. Black out every night. Terrible scare 1st morning at sea when "all clear" sounded, thought we had been hit. Getting tired of seeing water, 2 or 3 rough days, give lots of medication, enemas, etc.

We also provided support to the ship's hospital area, which had 12 to 15 beds and was equipped for emergency surgery, should something like an appendectomy be necessary. Our job even included giving enemas to constipated soldiers.

Fred and I stayed in the hospital unit as much as possible, as it was more comfortable than our quarters below. We traded hours of sleep and duty if we were not busy. Usually, we only had two or three people in the ward at a time. The air was fresher and less crowded in the hospital area than down below.

One soldier, whose baby face made him look more like he was 15 than 19, was being sent to Europe as an infantry replacement. This would be a very difficult assignment for any soldier because he does not have the benefit of going together with men who had become his "brothers" during shared training. The men of the units they join know the replacements are needed, but these new men reminded survivors of the band of brothers who died.

Gripped with fear, this young soldier on our ship was conscious and awake, but unable to speak or eat. We stayed with him night and day but could not get him to respond; neither could the doctor who tried daily to rouse him. When we landed in Liverpool on August 22, 1945, we saw him carried out on a stretcher that was brought to shore via a big crane. I assume he was taken to an Army hospital, although I had no information about him after we landed.

Before we left for England, we had a reassuring orientation to the kind of support we would get in our convoy as we traveled on the Atlantic, where there were reports of German Kriegsmarine U-boat activity. We also had abandon-ship drills on board, but our hospital duty kept us busy enough that we didn't dwell on what might happen.

Troop ships were in the middle of our 50-ship convoy with destroyers on the outside watching for U-boats, which traveled in wolf packs. Groups of U-Boats scouted for convoys, shadowed them, and coordinated attacks. Later in the war, the Allies had methods for fighting back against these wolf packs, thus better protecting troop ships.

22 August 1944

Arrived Liverpool, England 2205 [10:05 p.m.] First impression not good, but wonderful feeling to see land. Long walk down gang-plank to up pier, didn't think I'd make it. 12 of us had to load baggage cars. Red Cross women served coffee and donuts—wonderful! Departed Liverpool 2315 for Stone. Schaefer, Gray, Kerch, W. Rudy, and I in compartment. Very tired, but felt pretty good.

23 August 1944

Getting us, our supplies, and equipment off ship took time and was quite labor-intensive. We then traveled by bus to our headquarters in Stone Castle, where we were to prepare for entering France.

Arrived Stone 0315, loaded crap on our back once again. Capt. Tucek, O'Brien, and Tommy met us. Loaded in trucks and went to Hosp. For hot chow, good meal. To Redlands and finally got to bed at 0500. Up early to look over surroundings. Pretty good setup, grounds pretty. Old Bill caretaker. Amused at way people talk, island very crowded. Found out we had to leave for France as soon as we were ready.

We could see the next morning how wise it had been for President Roosevelt to create the "Lend-Lease Program" in 1941. It allowed the United States to support the Allies by selling, lending, or leasing equipment and supplies before we entered the war.

24 August to 14 September 1944

Back to work procuring and processing equipment prior to going to France. Saw Cheltimban, Cambridge, Coventry, Birmingham, Woverhampton, Honley, Stoke, and Trent. Countryside beautiful. Passes to Woverhampton, good dances. Honley—Pub, Red Cross, (stinky feet). Talk with Irish girl, British Wrens, etc. Red Cross in Stone—Clive and Kenneth. Eating at Howard Hall—Air Corp. Wonderful food. Pick up mail at Duncan Hall, met Harriet Crombecke's husband. Alerted for movement to France, wondering what's coming up. English money hard to get used to but had it figured out good when we left. Drive going good in France.

During the three weeks we were in England, I traveled around the country gathering the equipment and supplies we needed in France. It was a massive assignment considering there were 600 of us going in together but in different roles. We saw an amazing amount of equipment and material, which covered every bare piece of land. With all the American equipment, it was said the island must have sat a foot lower than before the war.

The poor British were on their knees—although fought on courageously. The fear of many Americans was that if Hitler moved as rapidly through England as he did through Europe, we would not be safe even across the Atlantic. Germany, we worried, would get to us eventually.

Having so many Americans in England was a mixed blessing for the British. The local people used to say of the Yanks that we were "overfed, oversexed, overpaid, and over here," a crack that may have started with Tommy Tinder, a popular British radio and stage comedian. At the same time, the British were said to be "underpaid, undersexed, and under Eisenhower." The English people certainly loved us anyway, knowing we provided the resources in equipment, arms, and men needed to protect them from and defeat Germany.

We never made it into London during those three weeks, as that city was a war zone that German airplanes hit with bombs and V-2 rockets. The Nazis claimed the Vergeltunswaffe (Retaliation) 2 rockets were in retaliation for Allied bombing of German cities and military targets. V-2 rockets were short-range ballistic missiles that specifically targeted London. Later, they aimed the rockets at Antwerp, Belgium, where much Allied equipment and supplies came into the continent for the Allies' use.

We left Stone Castle on September 15, 1944, heading for the Port of Southampton, where we embarked onto the many landing ships that took men and equipment into the beach at Normandy. Loading the landing ships took a massive, coordinated operation because we needed much equipment to make our landing and perform our mission.

> September 15, 1944
>
> Departed Stone at 0800 via motor convoy enroute to Marshaling area in vicinity South Hampton. Eating "C" and "K" rations. Arrived Camp Hursley at 2300, everything blacked out, robot bomb scare—several hits prior to this. Moved in hutment, officers and enlisted men together. Col. Sandy reported in and came back w/a report that had to be made up immediately. Colder than hell, laid and shivered all night. Slept w/ clothes on, very dirty and beaten up. Next morning drew more "C" rations, got to wash up, several of the boys put on shit detail. Alerted over loud speaker, hurried to trucks. Departed Camp Hursley at 0900 for Southampton harbor, beautiful day, drove on LST 509 and stayed in harbor rest of day. Sailed into convoy rendezvous area at 2200. Wonderful deal on boat, 120 GIs, plus sailors. Ate w/ sailors—turkey, steak, etc. Slept down on tank deck on litters.

London was 81 miles from us in Southampton, but we heard the Germans' screaming rockets and saw their tails of flame as they crossed the English Channel heading to London. The noise made it hard for us to sleep as exhausted as we were by our preparations. Our plight at that point was nothing like that of those living in London during the German attacks.

Once our armada was assembled, we were off to war, leaving at 8:45 a.m. on September 17, 1944, on a beautiful day. We traveled in a convoy of about 60 ships with Navy support and protection along the way. The many smaller ships were needed as they could bring in only 200 to 300 of us at a time to the beach and then went back to Southampton for more.

On the crossing to Normandy, we had two wonderful meals from the ship's mess. They were especially important because we did not know when we would get a hot meal again. Emergency rations—C-rations and later K-rations—would give us the calories we needed once in France.

Each ship had huge balloons attached to it by metal lines. The idea was that a dive-bombing plane would get tangled in the balloons. After one balloon started flopping around, a crewman cut the cable to let it go. "There goes $800," he said. It was a very large amount of money, as much as $10,800 in 2012 dollars.

18 September, 1944

Debarked LST 509 at 0230 at Utah Beach, funny feeling in stomach. Arrived bivouac area at 0315, very cold and dirty. Slept on bed of truck family style. Orchard. Hedgerows. Still eating "C" rations. Departed for 3rd Army assembly area at 1100. Much traffic. Terribly dusty. Lots of destruction. Went through St. Lo, Orleans, etc. Bivouacked for night in vicinity of Cloyes at 2255. Very dirty and tired. Slept family style again. Froze all night.

CHAPTER THREE

In the War

By the time our convoy left Southampton, England, for France on September 18, 1944, the Allied invasion that began with D-Day on June 6, 1944, had liberated Normandy, an area in northern France along the English Channel. Some 156,000 Americans, British, and Canadian forces landed that first day on five beaches along 50-miles of highly-fortified beaches. By June 11, 326,000 troops, more than 50,000 vehicles, and some 100,000 tons of equipment had landed at Normandy.

We had gotten our orders to go to Europe when the Normandy operation was at its most intense. By the time we landed, the Allies had fully occupied the area. Still, we saw how the fighting leveled the countryside.

With the liberation of Normandy, the Allies continued moving through France, regaining territory the Germans held since before the U.S. entered the war. The Allies reached the port of Cherbourg by the end of June, which allowed for 850,000 more Allied soldiers and 150,000 more vehicles to enter France and move on to liberate Paris. Historians described the Normandy landings as the beginning of the end of war in Europe.

It certainly was safer crossing the British Channel in a convoy on September 18, 1944, than it might have been earlier in the war, but it was not without danger. Our crossing was peaceful, although we certainly felt anxious about going to France where the war was very real.

My good friend Ralph Freed was at Normandy on the actual D-Day as part of an armored infantry unit out of Fort Campbell, Kentucky. He told me later that he was wounded in the hedgerows on the high bluffs above the beach, where the Germans were dug in with 88mm anti-aircraft and tank guns shooting down on the American soldiers below.

When a shell hit next to Ralph, his body filled with shrapnel. Initially paralyzed, he was evacuated to England and had several surgeries to remove the metal throughout his body, except for a hunk near his spinal cord. His doctors decided it was less risky to leave that metal in him and then scar over than to try to remove it. If they nicked the spinal cord in surgery, he could be paralyzed permanently.

Despite the severity of his wounds, Ralph recovered in December 1944 in time for the Battle of the Bulge, where he rejoined his unit. However, it took two weeks for him to find anyone he knew because the unit had suffered 80 percent casualties in deaths and injuries since D-Day.

Ralph's unit was among the many units marching into Germany, where the Nazis fought to stop the American Army at the Rhine River. Ralph's unit ended up in block-to-block street fighting in Cologne. The Germans were desperate to keep the Allies from crossing the Rhine at Cologne, part of which was on both sides of the river.

Just as Ralph and his two partners turned the corner of an office building in downtown Cologne, a German 88mm gun located at the end of a street shot. It blew off the head of the soldier on the outside of the three men, spraying blood on Ralph and the other GI. With the butts of their rifles, Ralph and his partner immediately broke a basement window of that office building and dove in. If they hadn't done that instantly, one or both of them would have been hit with the next shot. They remained in the basement for several hours until they could hear no more fighting and knew that the Americans had taken over the city.

Ralph, who told me that story later when he visited me during the Occupation of Germany, later died of a massive heart attack at age 52. I considered him a late casualty of war.

Battalion Organization

Our headquarters battalion had four non-commissioned officers, commonly called noncoms, who were in charge of enlisted men working under them, depending on their assignments. Fred served as the operations sergeant; Art Eden was the personnel sergeant; and Pappy Spanburger was the transportation sergeant, while I had five or six soldiers working with me in the Supply Department. I reported to Captain Arthur Tucek, whose responsibilities included being the Supply Department officer.

Heading our battalion was Lt. Col. Francis Sandford, an officer who did not stand on ceremony. He allowed us non-

Col. Sandford, Battalion Commander.

Technical Sergeant John Regnier, later to be promoted to Master Sergeant.

coms to develop a friendship that lasted lifelong. It was similar to the dramatized relationship between Radar and Colonel Blake or Colonel Potter on the television show, "M*A*S*H." Sandy, as we called him, was a civilian doctor who was called into the service after Pearl Harbor.

We had a remarkable amount of freedom and responsibility, having achieved the ranks of technical sergeant after entering the Army as privates. Each of us was awarded five promotions within a year to reach technical sergeant. Fred and I were barely in our 20s, the youngest of the noncoms, and still we supervised men mostly older than us.

21 September 1944

Up at 0400. Rolled packs in dark. Very cold and damp. Loaded trucks and trailer. Departed 0530. Arrived vicinity Hannonville at 1455. Bivouacked in orchard near 69th. Set up again. Heard first Nazi planes over that night. Trifle scared.

Our unit, which had been together since our training at Camp Forrest, Tennessee, was like one big family, rather than the kind of rigid Army battalion that was more common. Had a West Point officer been our commander, the relationship likely would have been different.

When my unit landed in France, we bivouacked a mile inland from the beach, though still within the wreckage of Normandy. In those early days, before our cook could set up his oven and scavenge for food, we relied on emergency rations—

C-Rations and then the improved K-Rations.

The Quartermaster is responsible for the quarters, rations, clothing, and other supplies in the Army. The Quartermaster Foundation, Inc., which supports a Quartermaster Museum at Fort Lee in Virginia, described C-Rations as consisting of three cans containing a meat and vegetable component and three cans containing crackers, sugar, and soluble coffee; it furnished 2,974 calories a day, including 114 grams of protein, and an adequate supply of vitamins and minerals.[10] The K-Rations, which were like a box of Cracker Jacks, contained a meat paste. The Foundation described K-Rations as having 8 units, that provide 8,300 calories, 99 grams of protein, but were slightly under the minerals and vitamins recommended by the Food and Nutrition Board of the National Research Council. They gave us nutrition and little else; certainly they were not steak dinners.

You can imagine how much we longed for a hot fresh meal instead of packaged food that came out of a box or can. While there was much destruction in the area, we knew some farms still operated as farmers were returning to them. We went to one farm, asking for eggs that we hoped to cook in our mess kits over a fire. Although we had been given an English-French phrasebook to help with communications, the farm couple simply did not understand our request. Finally, Fred sat down and pretended to be a hen laying an egg. It was probably the best laugh this couple had in years, thanks to Fred's acting. They gave us fresh eggs and some other food from their basement, which we thoroughly enjoyed back at our tent city.

The farmers of Belgium, France, and Luxemburg were eager to help us, as they saw us as their liberators. That changed when we entered Germany, where the people saw us as enemy occupiers.

> *2 October 1944*
>
> Stayed vicinity Hannonville. Getting colder. Started to rain. Getting very muddy and miserable. Went to Verdun a couple times. Nancy captured. Start of first battle for Metz. Receiving a little mail. Learning a few French words but "No compree boo coo."

Field Hospital

Our convoy left Normandy heading to Northern France, where we were assigned temporary duty to a field hospital, similar to the Mobile Army Surgical Hospitals (MASH) units that would be part of the Army medical operations. They were used beginning in August 1945 and then fully during the Korean Conflict and beyond; they were memorialized in the movie and television program, "M*A*S*H."

Camping overnight in Verdun, we found ourselves near a sea of crosses on graves for American soldiers from World War I. It reminded us just how serious war is.

It was on this journey through France to the field hospital that we experienced another incident of racial prejudice. Lt. Col. Sandford learned a quartermaster unit, typically staffed by

African Americans, was along the way. He made arrangements for our battalion to stop there for a hot meal so we would not have to eat still more emergency rations. We were all thrilled, except for some from the South who did not want to eat with African Americans, even though they were soldiers like us. One soldier went so far as to eat his K-rations by a truck. Why in the world would he turn down a hot-cooked meal? The rest of us were disgusted by his prejudice.

While the Allies thought the Nazis were on the run, the 3rd Army bogged down at the Maginot Line, the fortified French border with Germany that was supposed to prevent the kind of invasion the Germans made during World War I. France built a line of concrete fortifications, obstacles, and weapons installations on the Maginot Line in the 1930s, when it feared a new war with Germany. France also had a similar Alpine Line for fortification against Italy.

Germany responded by creating its own line—the Siegfried Line parallel to the Maginot Line "from the Swiss border along the Rhine River to the area of Karlsruhe and then northwest to Saarbrucken; it followed the Saar River to Trier and then paralleled the German border with Luxemburg, Belgium, and the Netherlands."[11] Once it occupied France after a six-week campaign, the Siegfried line was less important to Germany until after D-Day, when it began refortifying Siegfried in mid September 1944.

The fighting along the Maginot and Siegfried lines was bitter, with many wounded. Our unit was ordered to help the very busy 109th Field Hospital, although we were not trained for direct patient care. We were supposed to supervise ambulances crews responsible for moving wounded soldiers after their initial treatment at aid stations to field hospitals. In war, you do what has to be done.

> 2 October to 24 October 1944
>
> Left Hannonville at 1000. Arrived at 109th Evacuation Hospital vicinity Doncourt at 1030. Nice day. Lots of air activity. Beautiful day. Pretty good setup. Pitched tents and got settled again. 109th supporting XX Corp. (5th Division, 90th, 95th.) Starting to fight in forts at Metz. Rainy weather starting. Rain every day. Area getting very muddy. Started going to Operating Room at Hospital. Many casualties from Metz area. Watching lots of surgery. Met Roy Nelson from Rochester. Saw 18 year old boy, infantry, shot through spine, paralyzed from chest down, 6 months to live. Looked like Richard. Very sad. Assisted anesthetist on brain operation, 2nd Lieut. from New Orleans out of Armored Unit. First I had seen. Nearly passed out. Lasted 3-½ hours. Very serious.
>
> Watched P-47's dive bombing forts at Metz. Saw autopsy on young man out of Field Artillery. Terrible sight. Third Army pulled out of forts as they couldn't penetrate Nazi defenses. Casualties heavy. 150 to 200 operations daily. 6th Convalescent. 2 Robot bombs. Seeing many boys battered and crippled for life—gruesome sights. Good chow. Mail irregular. Surrounding towns very dirty here, manure all over. Mud knee-deep, feet wet all the time, very miserable. Pup

tent muddy every night now, not sleeping too good, burning candles to keep warm at night. Kerch and I got straw for tent, sleeping comfortable and good and dry, sleeping with all clothes on as it's too cold to undress and dress. Worst weather I've ever seen, everything bogged down. Not too many casualties now. Many of the fellows' pup tents flooded out. Terrible living conditions.

We set up our tent city in the middle of the night in a pasture beside the 109th Evacuation Hospital, which was near Doncourt. Cold and hungry during the night, we were eager the next morning for a hot meal. We were in one of two long lines of soldiers heading to the mess. One of the amazing and unexpected wartime experiences was running into a Marshall High School graduate, Bernie Juba, who graduated a year ahead of me and was assigned to that hospital. We found each other in line for the mess hall.

The surgery section consisted of big tents on a tarp floor with eight surgical tables. This surgery department was nothing like a big city hospital, but still offered excellent medical services that saved lives and prevented as many long-term disabilities as possible.

24 October to 5 December 1944

Moved from Doncourt to Thiacourt. Set up in much better area near St. Mithel Cemetery. Getting cold, still raining. Started working for Maj. Folkman, dentist. November 9th.

3rd Army opened big offensive on Metz. Most air activity I had ever seen. 1200 heavy bombers, 1800 medium bombers and fighters. Lots of artillery. Steady rumble all day and night. Watched B-17 crash in flames, crew brought to Hospital. Casualties really starting to roll in. 5th and 90th Division circling Metz. Fighting very hard. Gen. Patton gave orders—no speed limits, stop for nothing. Hard going for armor, too muddy. Doughboys doing most of work. Weather conditions miserable.

The 150 to 200 operations a day ranged from quick, half-hour procedures to operations that lasted for hours. I worked in the dressing and sterilization (DNS) department, serving as a runner delivering sterilized surgical packs and equipment to surgeons, as needed. We worked 12-hour shifts, a week on days and then a week on nights with no days off. We were "dirty" assistants, which meant we did not scrub to be in the surgical theater as the "clean" assistants did. However, everything that we took to the surgery was sterilized and then wrapped or in containers to prevent contamination.

24 October to 5 December 1944

Started to work in Dressing and Sterilization, right off Operating Room. 8 tables going day and night many bad cases (brain, laminectomies, amputations, maxo-facial, eye in-oculations, etc.) Working 12 hour shifts, one week days, one week nights. Kept very busy. Watching lots of surgery. Personnel to remember—Bradshaw, Kampf, Juba, Ralph

> Bennett, Miss Baily, Hart, Halloran, Quint, Fluff, Big Jane, O'Connor, O'Brien, Martin, Taylor, Cummings, Joe Wenis, Don Gereau, Bennis, Col. Moffert. Infantry broke into Metz. Overran a hospital. Hundreds of krauts coming through. Bad shape. No prior treatment. Many amputations. Many of our wounded also found.

Surgery was done and care given while U.S. artillery fired shells over the hospital and U.S. bombers dropped bombs on the German troops stationed in the fort area. As frightening as the sounds were from the bombs and shells, we looked on them as good news. We hoped every bomb and shell brought us closer to victory and going home.

Outside the surgical tents was a sheltered area for medical waste that included amputated limbs from soldiers which the Graves Registration Unit recorded with precision. Graves Registration gathered information about the dead and wounded to inform families at home. Their lot in the Army was very difficult; I did not envy them this duty.

This field hospital work was my baptism to the human wreckage of war. As I wrote in my diary in October 1944, "Seeing many boys battered and crippled for life—gruesome sights."

Most of us came into this war expecting it to be like past wars like World War I, where the two sides lined up and shot at each other from trenches. World War II was much different in many ways, including advanced weaponry and mobility, not to mention the eight to ten soldiers behind the lines who supported each man fighting at the front.

The weather turned nasty while we worked with the 109th hospital. It rained most of the time, which meant mud and lots of it. Conditions were primitive by today's standards, but we didn't complain because we knew how much safer we were behind the lines then in the actual fighting.

With all that mud, it was not easy to stay clean. The hospital had a laundry service for blankets, bandages, and other patient needs. We did our best to stay as clean as possible without getting fresh uniforms on a regular basis.

Our biggest objective in our pup tent was to stay dry under conditions in which mud was up to our ankles. Fred and I went into the village one day and bought a couple of bales of straw to put between the tarp bottom of our tent and our bedrolls. The straw was better than our bedrolls sitting right on the ground, but left much to be desired.

In addition to working in DNS, I was called into other roles at times. At one point, a dentist needed an assistant for his technician who was out ill. With on-the-job training, I mixed tooth filling by hand, and then I kept the foot-controlled drill going while the dentist worked. He primarily repaired teeth of soldiers with serious head injuries.

Among the most memorable cases while working in the hospital was the surgery on a soldier whose top of his head was blown off when he served as lookout in an armored tank. In that role, he stood with his head up out the column to alert the tank driver where they should or should not go, depending on obstacles. I was drawn to the young soldier because he looked so much like my brother, Dick, who was 11 years younger than me. Dick was too young for World War II, but later served in Korea.

I came into the surgical theater with a special lamp for the neurosurgeon. Being curious, I asked the surgeon if the soldier, who was from New Orleans, stood any chance of surviving. He told me that the brain was capable of regenerating itself, depending on the damage to vital areas. As the neurosurgeon siphoned out the injured brain matter, he answered more questions from me. It was good news that the critical threads were intact; which gave him a 50 percent chance at survival, although his quality of life would not be known for awhile. If he lived, the soldier would be sent back to a United States Army hospital on a hospital ship. Recognizing my interest, the surgeon said he could use my help during the operation to move the lamp where he needed it.

> *24 October to 5 December 1944*
>
> Offensive going good. Heavy air support daily. Metz completely surrounded. Good chow, mail service fair, Christmas approaching. Trips to Nancy, Toul, St. Maurice (old jeweler). Kraut SS troops feared to be operated on as they expected nerves to be removed, etc. Sleeping in ward tent now. Living quite comfortable. Mail coming in fair, but morale not too hot. Heard a few football games late at night. Have seen more broken, bloody, and battered men than I

> ever hoped to see—gives one a funny feeling in stomach and lump in throat, but am gradually getting used to it. Realize how lucky I am and thank God every time I see some of this stuff. Working pretty hard but don't mind as wounded have paid much more than I. Many Kraut SS patients, the bastards. Hate to see them get this good food and attention. French civilians visited us regularly. Little girl and boy who came out on Sunday. Came back the next Sunday with Mother to have their picture taken. Very cute little kids.

Several weeks into our assignment to that field hospital in northern France, I was working nights when many German soldiers were brought in for treatment. The Germans had left them behind in the forts after they fled. One of them brought in at 1:30 a.m. was a 22-year-old SS officer, whose right arm had been blown off by an artillery shell. With infection set in and tremendous blood loss, this man was ashen, clearly in very bad shape.

"For this man to have any chance of survival, he is going to need whole blood and need it fast," the American surgeon said to the surgical technician.

That was a very generous offer as whole blood was in very short supply and thus given only in dire situations. Plasma instead was more commonly used. The willingness of American doctors to do the right thing for an enemy was obvious.

"What kind of blood is it?" the SS officer asked in English, feebly raising his remaining arm.

"It will be the right kind," the surgeon said. "What's the problem?"

"If it is Jew or Negro blood, I don't want it."

The shocked surgeon pulled the sheet over the patient and said, "There are men who want to live more than he does. Get him out of here."

I don't know what happened to the man after he was taken out of the surgical tent, but I assume he died that night, as he didn't have much left in him to fight for his life. I didn't feel sorry for that officer, even though he was a young man. I couldn't believe he would be so blinded by hatred that he preferred dying over having blood from someone he thought unworthy.

As an ordinary Army soldier, I didn't initially know the difference between the Wehrmacht, which was the regular German Army, and the SS. Historians describe the SS as the original Nazi police who later became the super soldiers trained to choose death before giving up. They were expected to do Hitler's bidding even if what was demanded of them was wrong, unlawful, or immoral. You couldn't comprehend the fanaticism with which the SS were trained. I was appalled by what I later learned the SS did in this war.

That one German SS officer, who refused blood if it might have been Jewish or Negro, dramatized for me the type of training the SS troops received. As I later read, SS men had to be pure Aryan, which was the reason he refused to accept Jewish or Negro blood.

It's odd to think of there being rules of war, but there were, particularly for prisoners of war. The Allies took responsibility for any injured German soldiers when they became our prisoners of war. Our hospital treated anyone injured—including Nazis—because it was the right thing to do under rules of war and in a civilized society. I discovered later that the Germans did not share that sense of morality or responsibility at the Battle of the Bulge and I assume other battles.

Contacting Dr. Jacquot's Family Members

While I was at that field hospital, I sent a letter to relatives of Dr. Gastone Jacquot from Marshall, Minnesota, on his behalf. He had not heard from them for several years and worried about whether they survived and in what condition. He hoped I could visit them, but I was never close enough to do so. I contacted the family members and offered to see them if I got a pass, but they discouraged me. They realized that with food rationing, I might be more of a burden than help.

"Somewhere in France"
18 December 1944

Dear Mrs. Jacquot and Daughters,

You will no doubt be surprised at hearing from me, but when I tell you that I am a friend of your brother-in-law and uncle, Dr. Jacquot, you will no doubt understand. He has asked me to write you, as he has been unable to do so for the past few years. He wishes me to convey his greetings and best wishes and let you know that he and his family are well. Dr. retired from medical practice about 3 years ago and is now living in California, where he is enjoying a life of ease.

I will put his address on the bottom of this letter and he wants you to write him if at all possible. If you are unable to write to Dr., please write to me and I will forward the news to him as he is anxious to hear from you or about you.

I have been in France for several months and am a member of the liberating American armies. I hope and pray very much that you people didn't suffer too much under the yoke of Nazi tyranny and are joyfully looking forward to a new life of freedom. The French people have my heartfelt sympathy as I have seen and heard many things that make one's heart very sad.

I do not know what part of France you live in, but think it is a considerable distance from us. Let me know how far you live from Nancy and then I'll know if it would be possible for me to visit you. With kindest personal regards and the hope that this letter finds you well and happy, I remain,

Sincerely,
John Regnier

I received a lengthy letter back from the family, who were surprised to hear from a U.S. soldier. They wrote in French, but fortunately Bill O'Brien, who was in my unit, translated it for me. I sent Dr. Jacquot both the English and French version. These relatives told us about the German occupation, which was very difficult.

Saint-Julien du Sault, 14-1-45

Cher Monsieur,

I received your letter, but I am not answering in English, for it is such a long time since I have practiced that language and I no longer know it. I think you know French sufficiently now to understand it, or you will find a translator among your comrades.

I was very astonished, I assure you, on reading the return address of your letter on the envelope and the name of its writer. But your title of friend of my uncle explained all.

We wrote to him as soon as we were liberated, giving our letter to a member of your army, since there are some American soldiers, oh a very small number, who are around our region! We have received no response. We are very happy to have news of him.

California was one part of America which had always appeared to please him. He went there when he could. What became of Robert? I was thinking that one day, we would be able to see him appear at our house an American soldier. He was eight years old when he came to France.

We are going to write to my uncle. Although he will get it, you can tell him all the following, because your letter will perhaps arrive quicker than ours—that in spite of the terrible years of the occupation, lacking in liberty, restricted, we are in good health, and the morale has always been good. In spite of appearances, we did not wish to doubt France. As de Gaulle has said, she has lost one battle, but she has not been conquered; she has been betrayed, that is another thing; and now it is the relief of recovered liberty.

Oh! How we cried with joy when on the 22nd of August we saw the few American carriages across our city; all the flags were out, all the bells were ringing. We had not seen a great many things, because we are off the main highway, which necessitates a detour to go through Saint-Julian. And then, thanks to God! there was no combat in our immediate region.

We thank you for extending your hand in this gigantic readressment that we must operate. There is nothing but material ruin and broken morale, alas! Since you arrived in France, you can count for yourself what our country has suffered in its life work. What we must wish for now is a peace not sabotaged as it was in 18.

You spoke of Nancy. It is not in this region that we live; but it is between Sens and Joigny, on the Paris–Lyon railroad (130 Rue de Paris). We will be happy to receive you but, you know, the question of heating and food is far from being solved, and it will be necessary to content yourself if you come, with our little fire and our meager table. You will find us in the middle of moving for we have changed our house.

We congratulate you and thank you for taking part in the army of liberation. You must have had much work lately with the German offensive. When one thinks of all the blood spilled, all the suffering, the devils that are on the entire world, one can only condemn the one who brought about this cataclysm.

I send you, dear sir, our wishes for good luck and the same time our best wishes.

J. Jacquot

P.S. If I have written that we have seen only a very few American soldiers, it is not that I judge your army is not important enough; I wish to simply express my regret; in our country and at some distance from the highway, it is not passed often. I put, with my flag, two [American flags] where I wrote thank you. They have not been much seen. . . . From St. Julien, they would have had much success for, during 48 hours, our troops filed out, and following that it was part of Leclerc's division. This country has more opportunity!

In that letter, she referred to Leclerc's division, Commanded by French General Philippe Leclerc de Hauteclocque, which returned to France to fight in the final campaigns in the war.

Dr. Jacquot, who had visited these cousins with his son before the war, was thrilled to learn they were safe.

Preparing for the Invasion of Germany

After the 3rd Army finally took over all of Northern France, we moved to Metz, France, where we were getting ready for the 3rd Army to enter Germany. Our assignment was to provide ambulance evacuations of casualties from an aid station near the front. Now assigned to the 4th Armored Division of the 3rd Army, we arrived at Metz on December 10, 1944.

> *10 December to 19 December 1944*
>
> Battalion moved to Metz, 10 Dec. Much evidence of hard fighting. Wreckage, Kraut dead. Dead animals, many bomb and shell craters. Two forts still holding out. Set up in Petite Seminary, former German Headquarters. Building wrecked. Colder than hell. Didn't sleep good first few nights as artillery banging away overhead. Quite a bit of sniper fire at night. Civilians not too friendly. Last fort falls, everything quiet. Port of Clearing Co. Moved to Lauterbach, Germany on 17 Dec. supporting 5th Rangers and 6th Cavalry.

This border city, which bounced back and forth between being part of Germany and France over the years, was the last one liberated by the Allies. After World War I, it was part of France but then German annexed it in 1940 after it won the Battle for France. Metz remained with the Germans until the U.S. Army liberated it in November 1944 after a three-month battle. That long battle slowed the American advance on Germany.

Our quarters were in a partially-occupied Catholic Seminary building. I remember visiting with a couple of priests who lived in the seminary. When I introduced myself as John Regnier, they were excited and told me that there was a priest in that seminary of the same name. They would be happy to arrange my meeting him the next day if I were available.

Battle of the Bulge

I did not have that opportunity. It all changed—at least for a time—beginning in mid December 1944. We were ordered to Luxemburg and Belgium, our first war-zone experience.

Historians described the difficult conditions of this battle that began as winter set in. The Germans sent 200,000 troops from 30 divisions and with a thousand tanks from 30 divisions for a last stand against the Allies. Hitler's last gasp plan—reportedly opposed by his generals—was for this counteroffensive to destroy the British 21st Army Group and the U.S. 1st and 9th Armies north of the Ardennes, which consisted of 75 miles of dense woods with few roads. Hitler was sure it would work because Ardennes had been the successful battleground for the Nazis when they first took over France in May 1940.

When the counteroffensive began, the Ardennes was only lightly held by inexperienced and battle-worn American divisions "stationed there for rest and seasoning."[12] It was thought those soldiers were sufficient because the Allies controlled

France and the war in Europe was all but over.

Instead, Hitler ordered his army to drive through and retake the port city of Antwerp, Belgium, a critical port for bringing in Allied supplies and equipment for the retaking of France and Belgium. Not only did he want to prevent the Allies from getting supplies, Hitler hoped to get these materials for his own suffering troops.

Once that battle began, our orders turned on a dime early on December 19, 1944, when we moved out in the middle of the night. The 3rd Army moved at top speed to stop the German Army, a logistics challenge that included moving 150,000 men and related equipment within 24 hours over rough roads and in blackout conditions. The 3rd Army was to go back to Luxemburg to retake land there and in Belgium.

You may remember that scene from the movie *Patton* in which the general directed bumper-to-bumper traffic at an intersection where the massive amount of trucks, tanks, and other equipment were bogged down. It was a true story, one I remember personally, as we went through that intersection where several country roads converged for several miles in Northern France. Wearing his white helmet and a Colt 45 revolver on each hip, he waved us through with both arms. I remember feeling astonished and excited that this famous and colorful general was at that crossroads.

19 December 1944

Alerted at 1130 night of 18th. Something big. Messenger had to go to Lauterbach and bring Clearing Co. back. No

> sleep tonight. News of breakthrough by Germans a few days ago, but didn't realize how serious until now. Packed up and loaded trucks all night. Many rumors. Whole 3rd Army moving. 7th taking over our positions. Much excitement. Departed Metz 400 and proceeded on to Luxemburg City. Most traffic and equipment I had ever seen. Very cold. Roads lined bumper to bumper. Much anti-aircraft along roads, expecting air attacks. Orders changed about moving to Longway for night. Heavily bombed that night, lucky. Arrived in Lux, City at 1830. Very cold, tired, and anxious. Ate cold rations all day. Moved into schoolhouse with III Corps. Hq. For night. Got hot coffee, really tasted good. Enemy planes over all night. Much ack-ack fire and artillery. Slept on floor, slept very good as I was dead.

In his book *The Fighting Pattons,* author Brian M. Sobol quoted Patton's driver about that experience on a Sunday morning in Le Mans, France: "'Four streets came together at this particular intersection and there was a convoy on each street and traffic was blocked. General Patton got out and started directing traffic and in thirty minutes you couldn't see a vehicle anyplace,' said Master Sergeant John Mims. 'When the people were coming out of church and heard him hollering and cussing, they were taken aback, but when they saw who it was they burst out laughing. It was typical, Patton moving the troops himself.'"[13]

Our battalion went to Arlon, which was south of Bastogne

and just north of the Luxemburg border to provide medical support to the 4th Armored Division of the 3rd Army.

I felt so badly about the people of Luxemburg who thought they were finally liberated and then faced the Nazis' counteroffensive. They feared being conquered again by the brutal German Army. The women of Luxemburg were so happy to see the Americans that they gave us coffee and rolls in the middle of the night. On December 20, I noted in my war diary, "Civilians were ready to flee."

Surrounded by German units, Bastogne was under siege. We were on alert 24 hours a day. It was not comfortable trying to sleep.

With the city cut off by the Germans, American troops in Bastogne received supplies by parachute drops from the U.S. Army Air Corps (later Air Force). The parachutes were color-coded to indicate the type of supplies being dropped. I don't remember what the colors represented, but the idea was for soldiers to know which had food and which had ammunition or other needed equipment.

During the time American casualties were evacuated from Bastogne in Arlon, Belgium, one of our ambulance drivers brought me a couple of parachutes from the supply drop, which I later sent home. There is no way I could have imagined that my future wife, Eva Mae, would make Halloween costumes out of this life-saving parachute material that I had sent home after the war. I still have swatches of that old material.

> *21 December 1944*
>
> Enemy positions 2 miles out of town. Patrols into outskirts. Strict security rules laid down. Germans in G.I. uniforms in town. Anyone outside after dark unauthorized will be shot. Everything disorganized. Heavy enemy air attacks. Ration dump bombed daily, strafed 2 nights. Really froze in sack. Passwords changed every few hours. Snowing, very cold. Infantry having it extremely miserable. Heavy counter-attack started. Germans stopped and lines stabilized at last. Progress very slow as both elements and enemy very tough. Clearing Station set up to receive heavy casualties. Bastogne completely surrounded. 101st Airborne fighting magnificently.

The men of the 101st Airborne were among the true heroes of World War II. Their heroism was well known from the Battle of Normandy on through the war. They fought so hard to free Bastogne that they were dubbed "The Battered Bastards of the Bastion [fortification] of Bastogne."

After Bastogne was liberated, we saw just how leveled the city was from the bombing. It was hard to remember that it was Christmas when we saw the destruction, the many wounded and dead, including, as I noted in my diary, "Kraut dead piled up like cordwood around Bastogne." The outlook did not look very good, but the Allied forces were able to move out in great force once the weather cleared. I wrote, "Constant roar all day as they are really giving them hell."

Unexpectedly but quite happily, I was able to attend services, which were very important to me. They say there are no atheists in foxholes, and I agree. I really learned to pray in the Army in the midst of the horrors of war and tried to get to Mass as often as I could. That day, it was amazing to see soldiers dressed for battle at spiritual peace during Mass, despite hearing artillery in the skies above the church.

25 December 1944

Went to Mass in Arlon Cathedral. Artillery rumbling all during Mass. Very cold. Got turkey late the 24th for Christmas. Didn't expect to have it. Quite a bit of mail—4 boxes received.

Wonderful dinner, but otherwise the same as any other day.

26 December 1944 to 1 January 1945

Attack progressing. Gains slow and costly. Weather conditions still miserable. Kraut prisoner incident—Col. Sandy and Lt. Walks uptown, souvenir shop (Ann, Veronica, Sad Sack, Mama and Papa). Beer joints in Arlon. 17th Airborne brought up into line, also 87th Division. Special Service show (Bobby Breen, etc.). Supplies dropped to Bastogne garrison by parachute. 4th armored broke through to Bastogne. Ambulances and trucks sent in for wounded. Casualties heavy. Many wounded Krauts from Bastogne. Surgical teams sent in by glider before breakthrough. Much snow, very cold. P-47 crashed right out of town. Pilot brought into Clearing Station. Gruesome sight. Incident of fellows in weapons carrier who had 3 dead GIs, trying to dispose of them.

We made our headquarters in an empty hospital building. We were there to support the 4th Armored Division, whose job it was to re-liberate Bastogne. We continued on high alert day and night in Belgium because again we heard SS snipers were taking uniforms, dog tags, and weapons off dead GIs to get close enough to assassinate us. That was the most anxious part of the war for me, especially at night.

At first, the German Army made rapid gains in its surprise counteroffensive, but instead of breaking through the American lines, it only created a large "bulge" in the Allied lines, which gave the battle its name. The Nazis did not get as far as the Meuse River, which historians said was Germany's first objective in this campaign.[14] By the end of January 1945, American soldiers under Patton's direction had retaken lost land.

15 January to 27 January 1945

Still in Arlon. Everything going pretty good. Roads terrible. Morale pretty good as Russians are on the offensive. Buzz bomb landed in town, scared hell out of everyone. Visited 109th in France. A-20 crashed right outside of town. Several killed. Bodies badly mangled. Weather some better but still very cold. Getting ready to move. Drive going fairly well, but casualties heavy.

As we moved through Belgium, France, and Luxemburg, local people greeted us warmly, waving American flags along with their own and offering the American army anything we needed. It was relief to see us, they told us, as the Nazis returned and occupied their villages during the winter counteroffensive—after they were thought to be gone forever. For those who lived through 1940 in Europe, the fear of the Germans was all too familiar. Belgian townspeople told us they put away their Allied flags when the Germans returned. Police in Paris enforced an all-night curfew during that time.

British veterans waited nervously to see how the Americans would react to this full-scale German offensive, and British generals quietly acted to safeguard the Meuse River crossings. Even American soldiers who thought final victory was near were sobered by this last Nazi onslaught.[15]

General Eisenhower rushed reinforcements to fight the counteroffensive, with General Patton leading our response. As the military website noted, the American soldier, isolated in bitterly cold conditions with deep snow and without understanding the whole picture, still managed to have the resilience to fight on against the Nazi advance.

One of the most legendary moments in the war came in that battle for Bastogne, when German soldiers surrounded the city. Military historians said four German soldiers carrying a white flag walked up the road to the Americans with this demand from the German commander: "To the USA Commander of the encircled town of Bastogne: There is only one possibility . . . the honorable surrender of the encircled town."[16]

Gen. Anthony Clement McAuliffe, then acting commander of the 101st Airborne Division, gave a single-word response: "Nuts!" That one word inspired his troops in the midst of that battle and the Allies everywhere when they heard about that general's spirited reply.

Within days, Patton's 3rd Army arrived to provide the needed support. The army stopped Hitler's tanks just before the Meuse on Christmas Day.

"This is undoubtedly the greatest American battle of the war and will, I believe, be regarded as an ever-famous American victory,"[17] said British Prime Minister Sir Winston Churchill.

Again, at the time we knew nothing about numbers or the grand strategy of war, only that our combat troops were going through hell. We were only a very small piece of the whole: ambulance companies that evacuated casualties from the front-line aid stations to field hospitals.

We learned later that this was the most costly U.S. battle in Europe in terms of casualties. The Battle of the Bulge lasted for 44 days and involved hundreds of thousands of soldiers. During that time, nearly 20,000 Americans were killed and about 60,000 wounded, while the Germans took another 18,000 U.S. soldiers prisoner. British troops suffered about 1,400 casualties, while estimates for the Nazi deaths ranged from 70,000 to 100,000 depending on sources.[18] Estimates vary about how many Americans were involved, but it is safe to say that there were at least half-a-million troops—American, British and German—in this battle.

The horrific weather played a huge role in the injuries, as Reuel Long of Company E, 357th Regiment of the 90th Infantry division, described in a story posted on a website dedicated to Battle of the Bulge memories.

> *Our feet were becoming almost as big a concern now as the enemy, and during this period of time we started losing men we could not afford to spare to frostbite, trench feet, and frozen feet. We weren't getting our usual dry change of socks every few days, and it didn't help to bare your wet foot in below-freezing weather. So most of us tried to keep wiggling our toes while on night guard duty, or during periods that we weren't marching during the day. But we all soon became run down and tired due to the strain of combat and being outside in the cold for an extended period, so that many just gave up the additional effort to take care of their feet.*[19]

Decades after the war, when Fred and I had a reunion with Col. Sandford in 1996, he told us about his own encounter with Patton. All medical commanders were called to a meeting in Luxemburg, where he reconnected with a doctor who had been in medical school with him back in the Untied States. This colleague, who was a lower rank, was the commander of a smaller field hospital. He told Sandy he should visit if ever in the area. A few days later, right after the U.S. Army retook

Bastogne, Col. Sandford did.

After lunch, the other doctor took Sandy to see the men who had come in that day via ambulance. Thirty to forty soldiers from the Bastogne area were hospitalized with blackened feet so severely frozen that they were in danger of losing their limbs.

While the two doctors discussed cases, Patton and his entourage suddenly appeared in the hospital tent, demanding to know who the officer in charge was. Because Colonel Sandford had the highest rank at that moment, he saluted Patton and said, "I believe I am, sir."

"What are you doing for these soldiers?" Patton demanded, literally in Col. Sandford's face.

After Sandy explained the seriousness of the conditions of the hospitalized men, Patton barked, "Why didn't they leave the bastards on the line until something serious happened to them?" Paton then turned and left the tent, refusing to talk to any of the soldiers.

Sandford told Fred and me at our mini reunion that Patton shocked and appalled him, as he knew some of these men would lose their feet. Sandy was not one to swear, but he told us, "That was the only time I ever saw the man in person, and I never wanted to see that son-of-a-bitch again."

As the Allies took back more territory, we moved into northern Luxemburg, an area just east of Bastogne. We moved through several towns in Luxemburg, including Mondorf,

Our unit crossed the Rhine over a pontoon boat that the Seabees built for us and other units crossing. Reaching this point was a major accomplishment for the U.S. Army, although we realized we were moving into hostile territory. Photo taken by Fred Kercheval.

where we readied equipment for the invasion of Germany. That came on March 25, 1945, and we crossed the Rhine on March 30, 1944.

25 March 1945

Big day. Alerted for movement to Germany. Much excitement. Missed Mass for 1st time overseas. Worked all morning gathering up equipment and loading trucks. Transferred to 65th Group. Ate early chow and left at 1200. Rode all day and arrived 65th Group, Bad Kreuznach, Germany in

> evening. Very dirty and tired. Assigned mission of evacuating all VIII Corp. Divisions, namely 76th, 87th, and 89th, 6th Cavalry also in Corp. Big buildup for Rhine crossing. Convoys rolling day and night. Heavy air attacks on Rhine assembly areas. Sky completely lit up tonight. Slept at Group. XII Corp crossed Rhine at Maintz. 4th Armored advancing rapidly, pouring troops across 581st and 593rd Ambulance Co. Attachment.

Entering Germany

We left welcoming people in France, Belgium, and Luxemburg, who were so grateful that they gave us any kind of help they could. In Germany, we were the invaders; the occupiers, the enemy fighting their own soldiers. I'm sure the German people feared the Allied victory meant it would return their country to the kind of painful occupation they experienced after Germany lost the First World War.

When we arrived in Kastelleum, Germany, on March 25, 1945, we commandeered a house as our headquarters. "Kicked first civilians out of house," I wrote. "Very resentful. Unloaded and set up again. Scared to death during night as Kraut plane strafed right next to house. Aiming for gas convoy. Heavy equipment moving up all the time."

Here is how I described it in a letter home:

> *April 16, 1945*
>
> *Living in Germany is much different than anything*

we have experienced in the past, as previous to this we have been welcomed as liberators, which is far from the case here. The German people are very resentful, and one gets unwelcome stares from all of them. Many of them try to get in our good graces by pretending to be happy about our arrival, but past experience has proven that you cannot trust a German so they find few who will listen. I do not doubt but what there are a few who are happy to see us, but for the time being, they are going to have to suffer with the rest. . . .

One of the main things I have noticed is the abundance of young boys, ranging from six to twelve years old. They are a healthy, sturdy bunch of little devils, and of course, the first thing I think of is they are the nucleus for the next German army, providing of course that the Allies are foolish enough to leave loopholes in the peace treaty which will enable them to remobilize again.

We moved forward each day and, thankfully, the number of casualties declined as the battle for ground in Germany lessened. But those pockets of SS soldiers continued to be worrisome as snipers and saboteurs.

28 March 1945

Sniper shot GI through the head while eating dinner in next village. Brought in just when we were ready to pull out. Col. Sandy examined him and said he had about 3 hours to live. Evacuated back. MP's and GIs go to clean out the town. Moved to Boppard, Germany prior to crossing Rhine. Beautiful river. A little nervous these days. Advance going very fast. Big guns shooting over our heads tonight. Much racket. German planes bombed here the night before.

31 March 1945

Usual duties. House full of ammo blew up. Lots of noise. Don't trust anybody any more.

In one smaller town in Germany, where we set up for the night in an abandoned telephone building, our cook, Rudy Vasquez, set up a gas burner and cooked whatever he could scrounge up. Rudy "liberated" some chickens at one farm, managing to escape with his life after a farmer came at him with a pitchfork. He went into other empty homes, where he found potatoes and other vegetables stored in the basements. After cleaning up an old washtub, he cooked us an amazing chicken stew, the first hot meal that we had for several days as we moved through Germany.

Our convoy traveled mostly at night under blackout conditions—no headlights or other lights on to make it harder for us to be seen. It was also perilous because we could not see where we were going or know what was out there. The front windshield was taken off the lead jeep for better visibility in the dark.

After several jeep drivers were decapitated by barbed wire that the SS strung across roads, General Eisenhower ordered the motor pool to install steel rods on the front of all jeeps to break any hidden wires during the night advances. That simple change saved many lives. Sgt. Pappy Spanburger, who was in charge of our motor pool, made quick work of the installation of the rods. In his mid-30s, Pappy had managed maintenance in a large garage in St. Louis, Missouri, before the war.

We learned later that during this period in the war, Germany was so desperate for soldiers that it forced boys and old men into the Wehrmacht, the regular German army. Their training was much less than that of ordinary soldiers, let alone the elite SS, who were practically indoctrinated from birth for their roles.

After we entered Germany, I could not go to Mass as often as I wanted. Our battalion did not have a chaplain, so it was only if we were with another battalion that had a priest or in a town with a church still operating that I attended Mass.

> *1 April 1945 (Easter Sunday)*
>
> Couldn't go to Mass today. Boys from 87th Division brought in badly battered as they hit a mine planted by civilians or SS behind lines. Really made my blood boil. Three SS men attacked two 87th Signal Corp men and found them with Lugers. Took their guns, stuck them in their mouths, and killed them. One has to be very careful these days. Rations poor nowadays as all we get is C's and 10-in-1's. Stay pretty tired.

On April 2, my notes for that day included, "Roads full of slave workers." When I wrote that, I had no idea what it meant to be a slave laborer for the Nazis. I would soon learn.

CHAPTER FOUR

Unexpected Horrors

When we pulled off the road near Ohrdruf, we had no idea—no clue—about what we would see or where we were going. We had no idea that there were places like concentration camps or slave labor camps, let alone the killing factories in Poland.

We were just amazed to be in the company of three of the most important generals on the Allied side, along with other lesser-known brass. What was going on? We stood surprisingly close to these generals, something that is unimaginable in today's world. One photograph from that day shows Fred right beside General Eisenhower, whose head blocked my own as I was right there next to my friend that whole time.

Both very inquisitive, Fred and I recognized something very big was going on. We wanted to hear every word, although the generals were certainly more involved with other officers and in interviewing survivors. Eisenhower had a Russian translator with him who helped in the conversations with the few prisoners who managed to survive that hell on earth.

What we later learned was that Ohrdruf, a subcamp of the Buchenwald concentration camp at the southern tip of Traun Lake, was created in November 1944. By March 1945, nearly 12,000 prisoners were held there. Fearing discovery of what they had done, the SS guards forced anyone who could walk

General Eisenhower and other generals at Ohrdruf. Fred and I were amazed to see these generals with our very eyes.

on a 12- to 15-mile "death march" to Buchenwald, the largest of the German concentration camps. Many died along the way from exhaustion, starvation, or being shot by the SS Guards for not keeping up.

Liberation was not the right term for what we saw that day, as we were not the first to arrive and free the prisoners. But we were witnesses to the Holocaust or at least the effects of the Holocaust, which was very real.

Only a handful of the 100 or so who survived at Ohrdruf were at the camp when the U.S. Army arrived. They had been at Ohrdruf only a short time, which meant they were not so weakened by starvation that they could not get away when prisoners were rounded up for that death march. We learned later that Hitler had given orders that the SS guards were to burn as many bodies as possible in makeshift crematory pyres before the Allies got there. They doused the log piles with gasoline on steel railroad rails with bodies on top and set them afire. When the SS guards realized how close the Americans were, they ran from the camp to stay ahead of the war. They did not finish burning the dead because there had been too many. That's why we saw the remains of these bodies when we toured the camp.

What made our experience so unusual was being that close to the generals, which allowed us to hear their conversations. Nothing prepared us for what we would see and, even more significant, smell. Words cannot describe this breathtaking and unimaginable inhumanity, although I tried in my letter home on April 16, 1945:

> *[The slave labor camp] consisted of a couple dozen filthy barracks where slave laborers and political prisoners had been quartered. There were no beds, only straw mattresses upon dirt floors with no space between each individual nest of lice. The occupants had no blankets and sanitary conditions never existed. At the end of each barracks was a so-called latrine without any type of toilet facilities except the dirt floor. The environment had been and still is a perfect culture for almost any disease.*
>
> *The kitchen consisted of several large vats. Before the German SS troops evacuated the camp and had*

machine-gunned its occupants, a meal had been in preparation. The vats were filled with a horrible mixture of stew with two manure forks stuck in one of the vats. Near another vat was a pile of black, moldy bread. This vitamin and mineral-lacking diet had been the only source of food for months.

Something that I really admired about General Eisenhower was his commitment to tell the world what we had seen at Ohrdruf and later many other camps. He had the forethought to anticipate a time when there would be denials of the atrocities. His urging us to take photos helps me deny the deniers.

Our proximity to Eisenhower—no farther than across my living room—meant that we heard his actual orders to Generals Bradley and Patton. We overheard what they said when the body shed was opened to show the stack of starved bodies inside.

"This is the damnedest thing I have ever seen in all my life," Eisenhower said.

"Those dirty German sons of bitches," Patton added.

We were close enough to General Patton to hear his angry order to the men,"You've seen what the bastards are doing. Don't try to take those SS bastards prisoners. Kill them! Kill them! Kill them!"

Quick lime covered those bodies, not to make them disintegrate but to hold down odors that were so terrible that you could not comprehend what you smelled. Working in the hospital during the war, I saw many American casualties and even truckloads of dead soldiers during the Battle of the Bulge, but they were not like this. The difference was that soldiers knew the risks of war. We would learn later that the Nazis murdered millions of civilians in extermination camps and many others died of malnutrition and disease in slave labor camps.

Fred and I were in stunned silence as we took pictures. A short time later, we were deeper into Germany. In a small town where we would bivouac we noticed what appeared to be a small camera shop. After getting set up for the night, Fred and I walked downtown to check out this store. We thought we might be able to develop our roll of film from Ohrdruf. Fortunately, when we got there we found an Army photographer from the 3rd Army Headquarters, who was processing film he had taken in many other camps. He agreed to process ours and then gave me a set of many of his photos he had taken in Ohrdruf and other camps.

I have long regretted I did not get a copy of one picture that he pulled out of his breast pocket to show us. It was of General Patton urinating in the Rhine River. He had a bet with his fellow U.S. Generals that he would be the first to "piss in the Rhine." He called for a 3rd Army official photographer to document that moment to prove his claim to that honor. That was the same photographer who helped us. I have since found that photo.

We learned later that Eisenhower also invited journalists, members of Congress, and other soldiers to visit the camps so

A photographer we met in the German village shared a photo he took of General Patton urinating in the Rhine River. Photos were taken as proof of his Army had reached the river before others. (Army photo.)

they could bear witness to what they saw. Among them was CBS broadcaster Edward R. Murrow who broadcasted from Buchenwald on April 16, 1945.[20]

> *There surged around me an evil-smelling stink, men and boys reached out to touch me. They were in rags and*

the remnants of uniforms. Death already had marked many of them, but they were smiling with their eyes. I looked out over the mass of men to the green fields beyond, where well-fed Germans were ploughing.

I asked to see one of the barracks. It happened to be occupied by Czechoslovaks. When I entered, men crowded around, tried to lift me to their shoulders. They were too weak. Many of them could not get out of bed. I was told that this building had once stabled 80 horses. There were 1,200 men in it, five to a bunk. The stink was beyond all description.

They called the doctor. We inspected his records. There were only names in the little black book—nothing more—nothing about who had been where, what he had done or hoped. Behind the names of those who had died, there was a cross. I counted them. They totaled 242—242 out of 1,200, in one month.

As we walked out into the courtyard, a man fell dead. Two others, they must have been over 60, were crawling toward the latrine. I saw it, but will not describe it.

In another part of the camp they showed me the children, hundreds of them. Some were only 6 years old. One rolled up his sleeves, showed me his number. It was tattooed on his arm. B-6030, it was. The others showed me their numbers. They will carry them till they die. An elderly man standing beside me said: "The children were enemies of the state!" I could see their ribs through their thin shirts. . . .

We went to the hospital. It was full. The doctor told me that 200 had died the day before. I asked the cause of death. He shrugged and said: "tuberculosis, starvation, fatigue, and there are many who have no desire to live. It is very difficult." He pulled back the blanket from a man's feet to show me how swollen they were. The man was dead. Most of the patients could not move.

I asked to see the kitchen. It was clean. The German in charge . . . showed me the daily ration. One piece of brown bread about as thick as your thumb, on top of it a piece of margarine as big as three sticks of chewing gum. That, and a little stew, was what they received every 24 hours. He had a chart on the wall. Very complicated it was. There were little red tabs scattered through it. He said that was to indicate each 10 men who died. He had to account for the rations and he added, "We're very efficient here."

We proceeded to the small courtyard. The wall adjoined what had been a stable or garage. We entered. It was floored with concrete. There were two rows of bodies stacked up like cordwood. They were thin and very white. Some of the bodies were terribly bruised; though there seemed to be little flesh to bruise. Some had been shot through the head, but they bled but little.

I arrived at the conclusion that all that was mortal

of more than 500 men and boys lay there in two neat piles. There was a German trailer, which must have contained another 50, but it wasn't possible to count them. The clothing was piled in a heap against the wall. It appeared that most of the men and boys had died of starvation; they had not been executed.

But the manner of death seemed unimportant. Murder had been done at Buchenwald. God alone knows how many men and boys have died there during the last 12 years. Thursday, I was told that there were more than 20,000 in the camp. There had been as many as 60,000. Where are they now?

I pray you to believe what I have said about Buchenwald. I reported what I saw and heard, but only part of it. For most of it, I have no words.

If I have offended you by this rather mild account of Buchenwald, I'm not in the least sorry. . . .

Eisenhower had still another comment, similar to one I sent home. "We are told that the American soldier does not know what he was fighting for," Eisenhower said. "Now, at least he will know what he is fighting against."[21]

In my letter home, I wrote, "Any doubts that I may have ever had as to our reasons for fighting this war were removed once and for all after seeing this. When there is a nation, as strong as Germany was, performing such atrocities to human beings, there is no other choice than to beat them down and

General Eisenhower and other generals witness the piles of bodies on the makeshift crematoriums at Ohrdruf. (Photo courtesy of United States Holocaust Memorial Museum.)

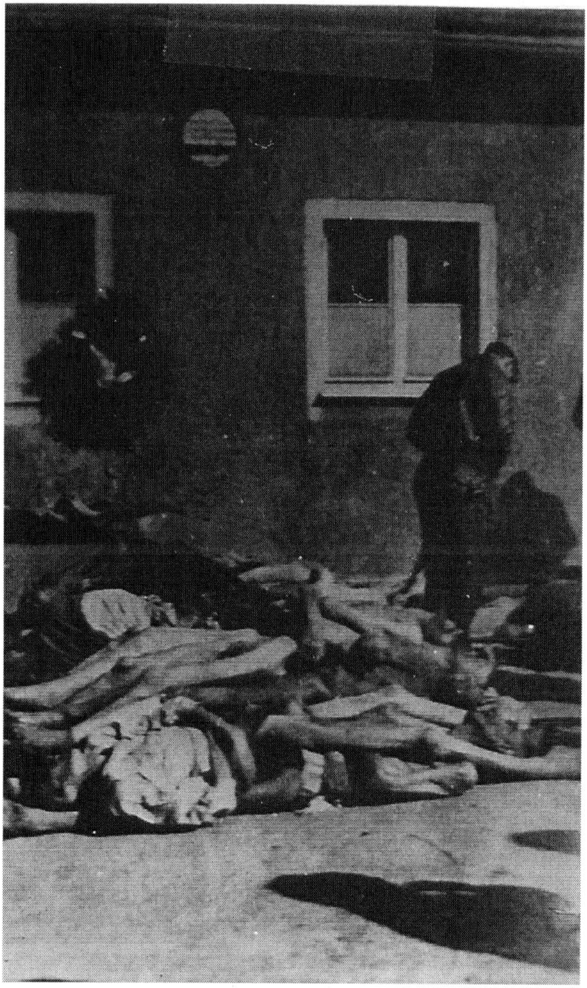

Bodies at Ebensee. (Photo taken by Col. Sandford.)

Sharp focus is not needed to see the horror of this photo that we took of the starved, naked bodies that were left in what became known as the body shed. Standing in front of that shed, we heard General Eisenhower say, "This is the damnedest thing I have ever seen in all my life," and General Patton say, "Those dirty German sons of bitches."

So much inhumanity. I hesitate to show the photos of bodies, particularly the ones that were without clothes and stacked in sheds. But they are a part of the record of Hitler and Nazidom.
(Army photo.)

Six bodies could be burned at one time in a crematorium.
(Photo taken by Col. Sandford.)

pray that they will be properly punished in time to come."

We also heard Eisenhower's order that local German civilians, including the mayor of Ohrdruf and his wife, be brought to the camp to see what had been going on in their backyard right under their noses. They and others claimed to know nothing about that camp, but they had to have smelled something very wrong. The odor was inescapable.

As one of the liberators of Ohrdruf later said in an oral history interview, "And the mayor comes up to him and says, 'well I didn't know what was going on.' So Colonel Sears says, 'you're a lying son-of-a-bitch.' He says, 'the smell alone will tell you what was going on . . . it was awful.' I can't describe the smell. It was so penetrating, horrible."[22]

The mayor and his wife were so devastated by what they saw that they went home and killed themselves, leaving a note that Pvt. Don Zimmer translated for the generals. It said, "We didn't know!—but we knew."[23] Zimmer, who spoke some German, was used as a translator until others with more formal training or native German speakers were available.

Zimmer said there was no way that the German people could be unaware of the evils in these camps. When off duty, the guards went into town to "brag, womanize, and drink," Timmer was quoted as saying, "so how couldn't townspeople know?"[24]

General Eisenhower also ordered civilians to give respectful burials for each body—or even partial body—found in those sheds, pits, or in those makeshift crematories. This is not something that we just read about in books; we heard him say, "If they resist, put a gun in their backs."

After becoming physically ill from what he had seen, the tough Patton refused to enter the building at Ohrdruf with the stacked bodies. Later Patton, who called that camp "one of the most appalling sights that I have even seen," wrote this in his diary:

> *In a shed . . . was a pile of about 40 completely naked human bodies in the last stages of emaciation. These bodies were lightly sprinkled with lime, not for the purposes of destroying them, but for the purpose of removing the stench.*
>
> *When the shed was full—I presume its capacity to be about 200—the bodies were taken to a pit a mile from the camp where they were buried. The inmates claimed that 3,000 men, who had been either shot in the head or who had died of starvation, had been so buried since the 1st of January.*
>
> *When we began to approach with our troops, the Germans thought it expedient to remove the evidence of their crime. Therefore, they had some of the slaves exhume the bodies and place them on a mammoth griddle composed of 60-centimeter railway tracks laid on brick foundations. They poured pitch on the bodies and then built a fire of pinewood and coal under them. They were not very successful in their operations because there was a pile of human bones, skulls, charred torsos on or*

Civilians were brought in to witness the dead bodies at Buchenwald. (Photo courtesy of U.S. Holocaust Memorial Museum.)

> *under the griddle, which must have accounted for many hundreds.*[25]

General Omar Bradley, who was more studied in his comments, said the evidence of starvation and bestiality "were so overpowering as to leave me a bit sick. . . . The smell of death overwhelmed us."[26]

12 April, 1945

Went to Ohrdruf Concentration Camp in afternoon. Most terrible sight I have ever seen. Hundreds of dead lying all over.

> Gen. Eisenhower, Bradley, and Patton, arrive to tour camp. Thrilling experience. We followed them around and heard their comments. Dozens of camera men taking pictures. Gen. Patton's comments when he looked in shed, also when departing. Didn't feel too much like eating tonight as I had a bad taste in my mouth. Saw civilians digging graves. (Near Gotha, Germany)

Ohrdruf was not alone in its horrors, as General Eisenhower cabled General Marshall on April 19, 1945:

> *We continue to uncover German concentration camps for political prisoners in which conditions of indescribable horror prevail. I have visited one of these myself, and I assure you that whatever has been printed on them to date has been understatement. If you could see any advantage in asking about a dozen leaders of Congress and a dozen prominent editors to make a short visit to this theater in a couple of C-54's, I will arrange to have them conducted to one of these places where the evidence of bestiality and cruelty is so overpowering as to leave no doubt in their minds about the normal practices of the Germans in these camps. I am hopeful that some British individuals in similar categories will visit the northern area to witness similar evidence of atrocity.*[27]

Still in numbed silence, we got back into our trucks and jeeps. That night none of us had the stomach to eat anything.

It left us in such a state; we couldn't understand how human beings could treat others that way.

We had seen many shocking deaths and injuries of American soldiers, particularly after Bastogne. Seeing truckloads of frozen GI bodies confirmed for all of us that war is a brutal, inhuman thing. But in war, soldiers at least had a chance to defend themselves. Prisoners in these camps were totally at the mercy of the merciless SS guards. Ordinary citizens had no ability to save or defend themselves. They were worked, starved, and brutalized to death. Little did we know, there were even worse camps than Ohrdruf.

At the end of the tour in Ohrdruf, Eisenhower had the presence of his very keen military mind to order two units be assigned to each camp as it was discovered. One would be a medical unit to meet the needs of prisoners near death. He wanted to make sure those poor starving souls did not have to scrounge for food after liberation. Army medics knew care had to be taken because survivors should not eat too much all at once, particularly the rich, high-calorie meals that we soldiers had and were eager to share because we so desperately wanted to help these people.

General Eisenhower ordered the infantry unit to put all able-bodied civilians into work gangs to dig up the mass graves and remnants from cremation fires to give respectful burials for each body—or even partial body—found in those sheds, pits, or in those makeshift crematories. This is not something that we just read about in books; we heard him say, "If they resist, put a gun in their backs."

General Eisenhower wanted cemeteries by the camps as a lasting monument to Nazidom. The infantry also was responsible for keeping order and preventing civilians or former guards pretending to be civilians from attacking survivors.

Death of Our President

> *13 April 1945*
>
> Heard news of President Roosevelt's death. Very shocked. Tried to listen to radio during day but couldn't. Getting ready to move again.

Although we didn't know it initially, our visit to Ohrdruf occurred on the same day that President Roosevelt died. We learned this as we moved in a convoy to our next destination deeper in Germany. A jeep marked with *Stars & Stripes,* the military newspaper, weaved in and out of the convoy tossing small bundles of papers into trucks. *Stars and Stripes* did not come to us on a regular basis, only sporadically if we happened to be where it was available.

This was a special edition, one that shook us, as I described in that April 16, 1945, letter home to my family:

> *It was a great shock to me when I heard about our President's death. It is a very tragic that he had to pass away before final victory is attained. I have no doubts but what the war efforts will go on unchanged, but it is at the peace*

Chicago Daily Tribune

AN AMERICAN PAPER FOR AMERICANS — THE WORLD'S GREATEST NEWSPAPER

"Hit Hard, Hit Fast, Hit Often!" —Adm. William F. Halsey Jr.

★ ★ FINAL

VOLUME CIV.—NO. 89 C — FRIDAY, APRIL 13, 1945.—34 PAGES — THREE CENTS PAY NO MORE

ROOSEVELT IS DEAD!

Truman Sworn In, Pledges War Success

NEW EXECUTIVE SAYS HE PLANS NO CHANGES

Asks Cabinet Stay; Takes Oath at White House

BY WALTER TROHAN

(Pictures on pages 2 and 3)

Washington, D. C., April 12—Harry S. Truman, one time Missouri farm boy, was sworn in as the 32d individual to become President of the United States in a simple ceremony in the cabinet room of the executive offices of the White House.

He completed the oath, which was administered by Chief Justice Stone, at 6:09 p. m. today (Chicago time), 2 hours and 34 minutes after the death of Franklin Delano Roosevelt.

Standing behind him was his wife, Mrs. Bess Wallace Truman, his schoolgirl sweetheart, who occasionally dabbed at her tear stained eyes.

High Officials Present

Deployed about him were members of the cabinet to whom Mr. Truman had broken the news of President Roosevelt's death and many high officials. Members of the White House staff peered in thru the three doorways of the room. Tears welled in the eyes of many of the witnesses.

With his face set in solemn lines, the 60 year old Truman raised his right hand to take over the nation's highest office. Chief Justice Stone delivered the oath from memory ...

TRUMAN FACING WAR, PEACE AND DOMESTIC TESTS

BY ARTHUR SEARS HENNING

Washington, D. C., April 12—The sudden death of President Roosevelt at Warm Springs, Ga., this afternoon brought the nation face to face with critical problems affecting the war and the peace and with possible changes in domestic policy of incalculable significance.

With Vice President Harry S. Truman sworn in as the 32d individual to be President early this evening the leaders of the government labored far into the night to gather the reins of administration firmly into the hands of the new regime.

Asks Cabinet to Stay

Among one of the first acts of President Truman was personally to request members of the cabinet to continue to serve for the time being, at least. It is believed that eventually there will be numerous changes in the cabinet.

Whether to postpone the San Francisco conference of 46 nations to construct a new league of nations to enforce peace was another question considered by Mr. Truman. He decided that the conference should go forward as planned and so instructed Secretary of State Stettinius, who is chairman of the American delegation and in charge of preparations for the conclave.

Stettinius later issued the following statement:

"With the authority of President Truman, I wish to announce that the San Francisco conference will open on April 25 as planned."

Expect Truman to Go

As the delegates to the conference from the allied nations were to have been welcomed in person by Mr. Roosevelt it is expected that President Truman will go to San Francisco April 25 to perform this function and launch the undertaking ...

THE 31ST AND 32D PRESIDENTS OF THE UNITED STATES

1882—FRANKLIN DELANO ROOSEVELT—1945

HARRY S. TRUMAN

Mrs. Roosevelt Gets News of Death at Club

ROOSEVELT FUNERAL SET FOR 4 TOMORROW; BURIAL AT HYDE PARK

Roosevelt's Health Failed Steadily Since Late in '43

THE WEATHER

Tribune Features

War Summaries

STROKE FATAL AS HE VISITS WARM SPRINGS

Succumbs After Complaining of 'Terrific Headache'; Had Been Sitting for Sketches

(Pictures on pages 4 and 5 and back page.)

Warm Springs, Ga., April 12 (AP)—President Franklin D. Roosevelt died unexpectedly today at 4:35 p. m. (3:35 p. m., Chicago time) of a cerebral hemorrhage.

Mr. Roosevelt's last words were:

"I have a terrific headache."

He spoke them to Comdr. Howard Bruenn, naval physician.

Presidential Secretary William D. Hassett said Mr. Roosevelt's body would leave here around 11 a. m. tomorrow for the 22 hour run to Washington. Mrs. Roosevelt arrived here late tonight with Stephen Early and Vice Adm. McIntyre.

Mr. Roosevelt, 63, was sitting in front of a fireplace in the little White House here atop Pine mountain when the attack struck him.

Bruenn described it as a massive cerebral hemorrhage.

No Pain at the End

The President's Negro valet, Arthur Prettyman, and a Filipino messboy carried him to his bedroom. He was unconscious at the end. It came without pain.

Mr. Roosevelt, in the third month of his fourth term as President, came here two weeks ago to rest.

Dr. Bruenn said he saw the President this morning and he was in excellent spirits at 9:30 a. m.

"At 1 o'clock," Bruenn added, "he was sitting in a chair while sketches were being made of him by an artist. (The artist was N. Robbins of New York City.) He suddenly complained of a very severe occipital headache (back of the head).

"Within a very few minutes he lost consciousness. He was seen by me at 1:30 p. m., 15 minutes after the episode had started.

"He did not regain consciousness and he died at 4:35 p. m."

News Spreads Rapidly

Only others present in the cottage were Comdr. George Fox, White House pharmacist and long an attendant on the President ...

table where the American people and the world will really miss him. The poor man has really been through some trying years, and it is amazing he held up as well as he did. He has earned his place in history, and I'm sure will never be forgotten.

FDR became president when I was in high school and the country was in the midst of the Great Depression. More legislation was passed in the first 100 days of his administration than at any time in history. With 25 to 30 percent unemployment at the time, the money the government spent putting people back to work was returned manyfold because people could then buy groceries, shoes, and other products again. When they did, it created even more jobs. Poor people revered Roosevelt as someone who really seemed to care about them.

Because of his involvement in Minnesota politics, Uncle Chick was able to hear a speech that President Roosevelt made in 1934 to honor the 50th anniversary of the Mayo Clinic in Rochester, Minnesota. Speaking about the world-renown Mayo Clinic, the President said:

Those of us who are concerned with the problems of government and of economics are under special obligation to modern medicine in two very important respects. In the first place, it has taught us that with patience and skill and courage it is possible for human beings to control and improve conditions in which they live. It has taught us how science may be made the servant of the

> *richer, more complete common life. And it has taught us more than that, because from it we have learned lessons in the ethics of human relationships—how devotion to the public good, unselfish service, never-ending consideration of human needs are in themselves conquering forces.*[28]

Moving Farther into Germany

Through April and into May we traveled through Germany, stopping in different towns along the way. We were in Apolda on April 14, Gossnitz on April 17, Hallfeld on April 21, Lauf on April 24, Ponholtz on April 27. There were times my diary noted how close we were to strafing Germany planes.

In Gossnitz, it was my turn to be charge of the quarters, which meant I stayed awake and on duty while the others slept upstairs on the second floor of this little hotel. We were in the midst of a bad storm, and I was hearing all sorts of strange sounds in the building, including sounds of rattling signs on the building. It was clear that if we were attacked, I wouldn't be able to do much. As a medical battalion we did not normally carry weapons, although we bent the rules and whoever was the charge at night was given a rifle.

I stood on one end of the first floor with that weapon watching for intruders. While our unit had control of the town, it was not impossible for there to be an SS behind the lines pretending to be a civilian or even an unhappy townsperson deciding to attack us.

That was the most frightened I had ever been in the war. I suggested to our commander that in the future we have two men up at night, rather than one. My recommendation was accepted. As I wrote in my diary, "It was the damndest night I ever spent."

My diary also included comments abut the reactions of townspeople. "Civilians really stare here," I wrote on April 14, 1945, about our move into Apolda. The 5th Rangers rounded up 500 POWs, including some dressed in civilian clothes. We set up in the hotel and visited with the owner, who had once lived in Milwaukee, Wisconsin. He still had beer in his taps, so we were happy.

> *15 April to 16 April 1945*
>
> Captured a couple prisoners. Tommy took them in. Food still very poor. Anxious to get fresh food again. Buchenwald Concentration Camp uncovered outside of Weimar. Worst yet. Gen. Patton makes civilians march through camp. Dying at rate of 350 a day. Civilians start digging graves. Armored spearheads nearing Czech border.

Ebensee Concentration Camp

Before the war ended, Lt. Col. Sandford was promoted to full colonel and transferred out of our unit on April 30, 1945. He was put in charge of 30th field hospital in Ebensee, Austria, south of Salzburg. We hated to see him go. He had been much more than a commanding officer to us; he was a father-like figure and even a friend.

We didn't have much time with our new leader, who came from the medical headquarters of the 3rd Army. We traveled south with the troops that took over Austria and were deep into that country in a little town north of Salzburg called Ried. It was a few days before the war officially ended in Europe.

The 101st Airborne Division of the 3rd Army liberated the last large concentration camp on May 5, 1945, the Ebensee Concentration Camp, which was located south of Salzburg in the Alps.

Col. Sandford's new hospital unit had the mission of saving as many lives as possible and arranging for the dead to be buried. His medical unit worked with an infantry unit assigned to recruit civilian workers to recover the bodies buried in pits. That strategy followed the model established at Ohrdruf.

Col. Sandford sent word to our battalion on May 8 about his hospital's new assignment. If it were possible for any of us to spend a day with him at his new assignment, he said we would agree that Ebensee was even more shocking than Ohrdruf. It was hard for us to believe that anything could be worse than Ohrdruf. A short time later, Fred and I, along with two or three others from our unit, accepted Col. Sandford's invitation and spent a day with him. This almost coincided with the official end of the war, Victory in Europe (VE) Day on May 8, 1945.

After going through Ebensee, we had to agree with Col. Sandford that this was worse than Ohrdruf. At Ohrdruf we saw no living survivors, other than a few who had been able to run off from the camp to go as far east as they could to get away from the German army. A few returned when the U.S. Army was there and described their experience in that camp.

4 May to 17 May 1945

Usual duties. Awaiting orders as to future assignment. Made many trips to Regensberg. Visited Col. Sandy at Ebensee. Went through Concentration Camp. Terrible sight. Lt. Lockard went to Paris for I and E school. Pappy arrived back from Riviera. Beautiful weather. Went fishing a couple times. Met little "Hedy" from Vienna. Talk with German civilian and his wife from Bremen and Vienna. Blowing up of ammo train on way back from Ebensee.

The Jewish Virtual Library described Ebensee, the last camp liberated by American soldiers, as "one of the most diabolic concentration camps ever built."[29] At the time of liberation by the 101st Airborne of the 3rd Army, documents showed 18,500 prisoners remained in the camp—in theory. Where were they all? At its peak, this subcamp for the Mauthausen Concentration Camp actually held 30,000 prisoners who worked at the nearby salt mine. Again, this was a picturesque little Austrian city in the foothills of the Alps near the base of Lake Traunsee and smaller Lakes Offensee and Langbathsee.

We walked through the barracks, which were designed for 100 prisoners per building, but at times housed as many as 750. We saw five terribly emaciated people in rags crammed together in most bunks meant for two or three. I saw some on these human shelves with only one survivor alive among the five and that one was far closer to death than life.

In one of the first barracks we entered, a man who was all skin and bones crawled over a couple of dead bodies in his filthy bunk to speak to us. I am unable to describe the smells except to say the stench was beyond anything I ever experienced or would want anyone to smell. This man, who looked like he was 70 years old, was a 30-year-old Jewish college professor from one of the Balkan countries.

"Help me. Help me," he pleaded in English.

All I could tell him was that a wonderful medical unit was taking over the camp and would get to him as soon as possible. It seemed so inadequate a response to this man, who was close to death as you could be and still be alive.

I hoped he was well enough to survive, but when we saw him, he did not have the strength to get out of that bunk. You felt so helpless in the face of such tragedy. The odor in that building was so strong, and you would not give what had passed as food in that camp to a dog.

Col. Sandford ordered medics to go through the barracks, sorting out the living from the dead. Even those who did not have a chance of survival were taken to the newly created tent hospital to be cleaned and made as comfortable as possible during their last days or maybe hours of life.

Despite the tremendous efforts of the 30th Field Hospital, Col. Sandford told us they were dying at the rate of 150 to 200 a day. These camps had so much disease, including typhus and tuberculosis in addition to the starvation, that it is a wonder any survived at all.

These survivors were so hungry, so starved, but they could not digest the very calorie-rich Army emergency rations we all wanted to give them. American soldiers learned the hard way—through these deaths—that our emergency rations that were a barely passable diet for us could kill these survivors.

Austrian civilians were ordered to help with this operation as well, as Eisenhower insisted these bodies—including those in mass burials—get as much respect as possible in individual burials.

I learned later that Jews represented about a third of the inmates for most of Ebensee's history, although at liberation the percentage rose to 40 percent. Ebensee then had prisoners of 20 different nationalities, as well as prisoners of war, political prisoners, criminals, Russians, Poles, Czechoslovaks, and Gypsies. Jews, however, "were treated more harshly than other prisoners," according to the Jewish Virtual Library.

Among the survivors at Ebensee were four Jewish doctors, who Col. Sandford told us made themselves invaluable to the American medics because they spoke multiple languages. These doctors, who had been in the camp a relatively short period of time, were able to communicate with both the Americans and the prisoners. Also in the camp was an Austrian nun who volunteered to help our Army nurses, who had similar communications problems with the survivors.

An Austrian nun volunteered to help nurse survivors and translate for the nurses. (Photo taken by Col. Sandford.)

Jewish doctors helped translate for U.S. doctors and other soldiers caring for survivors. (Photo taken by Col. Sandford.)

I read that 6 to 8 million Jews likely died in Europe during World War II, along with another 4 to 5 million non-Jews. The exact number will never be known because so many bodies were cremated or buried in yet-to-be-discovered graves. It is still hard to believe what we saw in the first and last camps liberated by the Americans (Ohrdruf and Ebensee).

In his book called *The Other Kingdom,* David Housett quoted a former slave laborer who described life in one of these camps.

> *Men who bear within them faiths uprooted and dignities undone. An entire race of men naked. Inwardly naked, stripped of all culture, all tradition, armed with spades and picks, mallocks and sledge hammers, chained to rusty ore cars, grubbers of salt, sweepers of snow, mixers of cement; a people gnawed by the lash, haunted by thirst, obsessed by the paradise of long-forgotten foods. The intimate gnawing of degradations. An entire people adrift on the stream of time.*[30]

Growing up near Marshall, Minnesota, I knew one Jewish family in town, who owned the Marshall Food Company. This fruit and vegetable business supplied all area grocers, including Economy Foods, where I worked in high school part-time and later for a year before I went to business college. The family son, Melvin, was in my grade at Marshall High School, so we were friends. He was just a classmate; we didn't frame our feelings about friends on their nationality, race, or faith.

Wherever we traveled in the last weeks of the war, we saw many emaciated people on the roads, desperate to get away from the hellholes where they had barely survived. I saw one who carried his totally infected and useless arm in his other. This man was just trying to go west toward the liberated portions of Germany. We directed anyone in dire need of medical care to where they could find Army medics. We couldn't do much to help their medical needs as we were in transit.

When we had the opportunity to hear stories of displaced persons, we noted their determination to get back to their hometowns in the hope of finding loved ones alive. Most, we learned later, would find no homes to return to and that their family members had been killed in camps like the ones where they had been slaves.

16 June 1945

Many Jews around here from Concentration Camps.
All want to come to America.

CHAPTER FIVE

The War in Europe Ends

8 May 1945

War ended. Waiting for official announcement.

Looking back, my diary entry for the end of the war seemed so understated about what we felt across Europe—at least on the Allied side. Our work was not done, of course. There was the occupation for as long as needed in Germany to return that country to civilization, something I was not sure was possible after all the horrors I had seen.

Somewhere in Austria
6 May 1945

Dearest Mother, Dad, and All,

Just another short letter to let you know that I'm still in good shape and things are going OK. The war is just about completed in this part of the world and the final announcement should come soon. It has been a long, drawn-out affair, but considering the job that has been done, it didn't take very long. Despite everything that we have gone through, it has been a very meaningful education and experience for many of us, and I'm sure will never be forgotten. War is a cruel and destructive evil, and I hope there will never have to be another one. I'm sure Germany will be very meek for many, many years as they are really whipped this time and I don't mean maybe. Every square inch of their damn country will have been conquered so they can never have an excuse for quitting this time.

Well, folks, now that we are in Austria, this makes the 6th foreign country I've seen: England, France, Luxemburg, Belgium, Germany, and Austria. When we boarded the train at Camp Fairest to start on our long journey, I never dreamed that we would cover the territory that we have, as I really never expected to get out of France before they gave up, but such is war and the army. Mother, I've received 2 of your April letters recently, and I must say I was extra glad to receive them as I hadn't heard for some time. I'm glad to hear that you are all well and that things are going OK. Good-bye for now and I'll write again soon, after victory I hope.

All my love,
John

A number of the men in my unit received the Bronze Star, which was created in February 1944 by President Roosevelt through executive order. It was an individual award for bravery, acts of merit, or meritorious service. It remains the fourth highest award a military serviceman can earn in combat operations and the ninth highest award in the military overall.

Sgt. Campbell was honored on May 8, Sgt. Kercheval on May 19; me on May 22; and Frank Johnson, who worked in various departments, on May 26. Col. Sandford previously had gotten the recognition in March, as had Captain Zimkowski, who was in charge of operations of our battalion; and Corp. Gray, who was Col. Sandford's jeep driver. We felt appreciated when we received these honors "for meritorious service in connection with military operations against an enemy of the United States" during our overseas duty in France, Luxemburg, Belgium, Germany, and Austria.

Most of all, we wanted to survive the war and get home.

After the war ended, I was among the 9 million troops the U.S. had in Europe. I was 23 years old, single, and had been in Europe for more than year. Others were older, had families, and had been in the war longer.

The federal government created a point system, one I thought was very fair, to get soldiers back to the United States who fought the longest and hardest. To be among the earliest heading home, soldiers needed 85 points, and I had about 55. Points were earned this way:

- Each month in service since September 1940 earned 1 point.
- Each month in service overseas gave an additional 1 point.
- Combat award (including medal and battle stars) provided 5 points.
- A dependent child under 18 added 12 points.

Those of us with 50 to 60 points were told we would be assigned to new units in France to prepare for the invasion of Japan before the end of 1945. While we might get passes periodically that allowed us to leave our units, we would not get a formal furlough that might allow us to visit family.

"Looks like Pacific for us before long," I wrote in my diary in mid-June.

We had no idea what the war plans were at the time; no ordinary soldier would. We just continued to work in our assigned roles in our medical battalion, trying to keep up our morale after VE Day.

"Prisoners were pouring in by the thousands," I wrote in my diary on May 7, 1945.

Germany was divided into four zones administered by Russia, France, England, and the United States. Most German soldiers wanted to become our POWs, rather than Russia's. That country showed no mercy to German prisoners because the Nazis brutalized Russian soldiers.

Weekend Passes

We were given passes after hostilities ended in Europe before we were to be reassigned for the invasion of Japan. After the long war, General Eisenhower wanted the troops to have as many opportunities for sightseeing in Europe as possible.

Fred and I were among a half dozen of men from our unit who took an Army Jeep on a scenic ride 45 miles southwest of

Ried, Austria, to tour Berchtesgaden, Hitler's Mountain Retreat in Bavaria. In some ways, it was like Camp David, the retreat that presidents use in the United States.

The town near Berchtesgaden, located in a valley in the Alps, was not bombed. The same could not be said for Hitler's retreat, which was located about 5,000 feet up the mountain from the town. It consisted of a couple of dozen buildings, along with an underground city. By the time we arrived, this beautiful haven for Hitler and other top Nazis had been severely damaged by the U.S. Army Air Corps.

In addition to Hitler's home, Martin Bormann and Joseph Goering had large houses in the complex. As head of the Party Chancellery and private secretary to Adolf Hitler, Bormann was always at Hitler's side after Rudolf Hess, then deputy fuehrer, flew to Scotland to negotiate a personal peace with Great Britain in 1941—and was then imprisoned for the rest of his life. Bormann was believed to have taken cyanide in 1945 rather than be captured. He was the one who gave Hitler's orders at meetings or via telephone. Goering was an early Nazi military leader, commander of the Luftwaffe, founder of the Gestapo, president of the Reichstag, Prime Minister of Prussia, and Hitler's designated successor.

Here's how I described the three homes in a May 31, 1945, letter to my family:

May 30, 1945

Goering's is the smallest of the three, and was very elaborate and well furnished. He had enough empty bottles

Fred and I were able to get a weekend pass after the war ended in Europe to Berchtesgaden, Hitler's Mountain Retreat in Bavaria. I'm shown holding a sign indicating where we were. (Photo by Fred Kercheval.)

This photo shows the damage Allied bombing did to Hitler's compound.

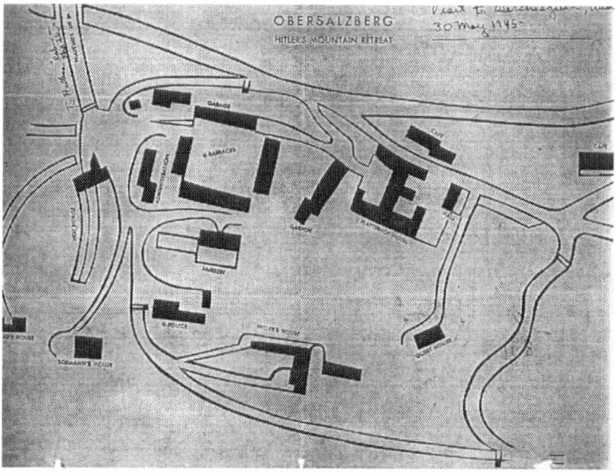

This map shows the buildings in Hitler's retreat.

in his wine cellar to fill a good-sized truck, so one can see that he was never thirsty. The kitchen is equipped with every modern convenience imaginable. There is still quite a bit of food in the kitchen.

Bormann's home (he is the one who succeeded Hess) is really the best of the three, I think, and seems to have been the most extravagantly furnished of the bunch. The woodwork and flooring are beautiful, and the bathroom fixtures are some of the best I've ever seen.

Hitler's home is by far the largest of the bunch and looks more like a public building than a private home. The laundry room and kitchen have enough equipment in them to take care of two hundred people rather than one. Boy, are they equipped! His living room is about the size of a small auditorium and has a mammoth bay window and balcony, from which you get a wonderful view of the snow-capped Alps in the distance. It is evident that he did lots of entertaining, as there are numerous guest rooms, bathrooms, etc. His house is the most heavily damaged of the bunch and has been pretty well burned out. It really gave me a funny feeling to rummage around in their private homes, and I know it is something that I will always remember.

I found Goering's to be the most interesting as it mostly had escaped being bombed. We saw leftover food on dishes on the kitchen table, evidence of how quickly he must have had to get away for fear of the Allies' advance.

In my later reading, I learned the motivation for getting away quickly may have been the expectation of War Crimes Courts to be established by the Allies. After the war ended, the U.S. tried leading Nazis who had been taken prisoner. The best known was at Nuremburg, where the Nazi leadership was taken, but trials also were held in other places, including Dachau. Goering was tried at Nuremburg and found guilty of war crimes. He was sentenced to death by hanging, but took cyanide the night before he was to be executed.

We also saw Hitler's Eagle's Nest on the mountain peak, but unfortunately could not reach it because the elevator was not working that day. Although we did not get to the top, we could tell Hitler must have had a magnificent view for miles over the mountaintops from his rarely-used home. We did learn there that the Eagle's Nest had been a place where leaders of the Axis powers met at times to plan war strategy.

A military police officer (MP) stationed at the elevator gave us a brief history lesson. He said 3,000 slave laborers had worked for two to three years to dig the elevator shaft for the lift to Hitler's cabin in the sky. He also told us he had been on duty when Gen. Eisenhower arrived. This MP heard the outraged Eisenhower's reaction to a sign that said, "This elevator is for field grade officers only," meaning majors, colonels, and generals.

"Who the hell put up that sign?" Eisenhower demanded to know.

"I did, sir," said the general escorting him. "There are so many people coming here that the line is so long that we had to control the use of the elevator."

Eisenhower immediately ordered the sign's removal and said with the war over, there should be no rank favoritism. Instead, he wanted as many troops as possible to see this place no matter their rank. GIs, who heard Ike, cheered, this MP told us.

The MP said many soldiers suggested that if it had been General MacArthur who discovered the sign, he would have replaced it with one that said, "Generals only."

The complex's underground city had tunnels connecting buildings and huge storehouses with enough supplies to last a year. Hitler reached his cabin by traveling several miles through the tunnels and then taking an elevator up to the mountaintop. As I wrote to my family, "This is really a marvelous feat of engineering, and one can't help but admire it."

The compound also included barracks for elite SS guards plus a building for female companions and a nursery. Nothing was spared in maintaining the morale of the chosen few who guarded the Hitler mob. Fred and I each had a photo taken on the back patio of Hitler's house.

"All in all this was the most interesting thing that I have seen over here and I've very thankful that I had the opportunity to visit this spot," I wrote my family. "This is really a historic spot as it was the heart of Nazism and all their evil plans. The 101st Airborne Division is occupying and guarding this whole area so they should be able to get some excellent souvenirs."

One of those souvenirs that I found didn't make it home. When we were in Goering's house, I spotted a Berlin telephone directory under a telephone in the lobby area. Inside were notes that Goering apparently had written in it, all in German. I tore the first couple pages out of the book, but made the mistake of including them in my letter home, asking my mother to save them for me. Even though the war was over, the censor wanted those pages more than I did, as they were not in the letter to my mother when it arrived. I often regretted I didn't stick those pages in my duffel bag and carry them home myself.

Occupation Duty

During occupation, our battalion headquarters assignment worked with two German Army hospitals that were similar to our Veterans Administration hospitals. Wounded German soldiers were technically prisoners of war whose care we were responsible for under the rules of war. Our headquarters was in Türkheim in Bavaria, about an hour west of Munich.

Little kids frequently came around U.S. soldiers, hoping for sweets. I was a sucker for little kids, giving them treats or something from the mess because I knew they were hungry and could always use more food.

That's where I met Franz, a refugee along with his mother from a village in eastern Poland that was caught between the Russian and German lines. The mother, son, and Franz's father hid in the basement of their home when Russian and German artilleries fought in and near their villages. When a shell hit their house, the father died and the boy had a leg blown off just below the knee. The mother wasn't sure whether it was a German or Russian shell.

Somehow through the underground Franz and his mother managed to get to Bavaria as refugees during the Nazi regime. He was a very happy little boy of 5 or 6 with a big smile on his face, despite having to scoot around on crutches.

When I learned one of the hospitals we were involved with had a large prostheses department, I communicated with Franz's mother to see if she were interested in having me contact that hospital about making an artificial leg for Franz. Of course she was pleased by that possibility.

The hospital was not supposed to care for civilians, but they responded well to reasonable American requests. The staff was happy to honor an American request to create an artificial limb for Franz. I also asked a Türkheim tailor to make him a suit, which he did. Franz was an even happier boy with a new suit and a leg that allowed him to move faster and more smoothly without a crutch.

I lost track of him when our unit was sent to Pilsen, Czechoslovakia, on October 7, 1945. The hospital there was in operation, but there was not much work for me; I hated to go in the wrong direction—away from home not toward it.

In my diary, I wrote about "good parties every night" and meeting a Russia girl named Katty, who was born in Kiev and lived in Prague for four years and Pilsen for six months. She was

During the occupation, I had the opportunity to share food with kids I knew were hungry. I also helped Franz by getting him a prosthetic leg and a new suit. (Photo by Fred Kercheval.)

the first Russian civilian I met, and like so many people I met in the aftermath of the war, her goal was to get to America.

I don't know what happened to her, as I was ordered back to Türkheim a week later on October 14, 1945, to join the 581st. Lt. Lockhart, whom I had worked with earlier in the war, had lost most of his key people by that time, so he asked for me to return to his ambulance company, which I did and served as a master sergeant, the highest non-commissioned officer below an officer.

We also met a young Russian soldier who showed up during the occupation in Türkheim. He didn't dare go back to Russia because military officers had made it clear that any soldier taken as a POW would be jailed for life. That was their way to scare soldiers to keep fighting to the bitter end. That was why he intended to go west, hopefully reaching the United States.

He was a nice guy, so we turned him over to the mess sergeant to work in exchange for food and a place to stay. The sergeant called him Charlie, which was much easier to pronounce than his own name. He stayed for several weeks, and then I assume he headed west.

Also during the occupation, we had a pass to visit Paris, thanks to a lottery pass system that Fred and I both won. We took a long, miserable train ride to Paris on July 19, 1945, eating donuts and drinking coffee provided by a Red Cross Club Mobile. After checking in at the Hotel Royal Astoria on 173 Rue de Lafayette, we cleaned up and headed downtown to see a Tunisian exhibit and then a GI nightclub.

French tour buses available to the many GIs visiting Paris helped us get on to see the sites; we didn't need tickets or reservations. Included on that tour was the Cathedral Madeline and the Follies Bergere in a show at the Olympia Theater. We were back to the hotel by midnight, stopping on the first floor to talk with the hotel clerk about life under the Nazis. The next day we went downtown again, as my diary shows.

22 July 1945

Slept until 0900. Ate breakfast. Called Lt. O'Brien and he

> came out to see us. We also went shopping on Rue de la Paix, walked down the Champs Elysees, visited an SS War Crimes exhibition and then had dinner at the Hamburger Club before sitting at an outdoor café drinking wine. We caught a B-17 military back to an airstrip near Lindsborg. From there, we caught a ride to Türkheim with 674th Weapons Carrier, arriving in time for evening chow in the mess hall.

While we were in Paris, we mentioned that we were not looking forward to the long, hot train ride back to Germany. A GI told us that we might be able to catch a ride in a U.S. military airplane leaving from Orly Field, the airport in Paris. On the morning we were scheduled to go back to Germany, we talked to crews of various planes preparing to leave. The first few planes were going to places like Italy, Africa, and England. Then we found a B-17 bomber about to leave for Germany. That crew was happy to take us on board. Taking seats in the nose of the plane for the best view, we were pleased to return in two hours instead of an all day journey to Landsberg, Germany, about 12 miles from our destination in Türkheim. Then we got a ride on a 674th Weapons Carrier to Türkheim. All in all, it was a memorable trip.

The Pipeline Home

When Japan formally surrendered on September 2, 1945, after those two atomic bombs were dropped, we felt tremendous relief. It was like being released from a steel trap. That was the happiest part of World War II for those of us in Europe. After that, we knew we would get in the pipeline to go home.

Little was known about atomic bombs, which were highly secret. At the time, we were pleased with President Truman's use of the bomb because it ended the war. I remember hearing him saying later in a speech on August 9, 1945, that "The atomic bomb is too dangerous to let loose in a lawless world."

In early November 1945 on the last day before I was to move to another assignment, I received a call to send two ambulances to Dachau, Germany, to pick up seven SS officers who had been convicted and sentenced to death for their roles in the Malmedy Massacre. They had chosen hanging over a firing squad.

At the time, I did not know about the Malmedy Massacre, but what I've learned over the years is nothing short of appalling. It was another insight into the SS mind, as I had gained in that experience at the field hospital caring for SS officers and soldiers left behind during the Battle of the Bulge.

Once enemy soldiers became our prisoners of war, we felt it our responsibility under the rules of war to care for them as we would our own. And we did, even if it meant giving whole blood to that SS officer, when we didn't even have enough for our own injured. It was the right thing to do, and the surgeon's response was correct as well. He said others wanted to live more than this SS officer who did not want blood if it possibly came from a Negro or Jewish donor. I'm sure the medical staff had no idea who donated that blood; it was only important that it be the right blood type for a patient.

But what the Germans did to prisoners of war was beyond any semblance of humanity. They certainly shot, tortured, and worked to death millions of Russian POWs in violation of rules of war after World War I.

According to the U.S. Holocaust Museum, 2 million of the 3.3 million Soviet soldiers in German custody had died by January 1942 from starvation, exposure, disease, or shootings.[31] The Germans claimed that they did not have to abide by the rules of war because the Soviet Union did not ratify them in 1929. It also had not ratified the 1907 general rules of law either. "Technically both nations, therefore, were bound only by the general international law of war as it had developed in modern times. Yet even under that law, prisoners of war were to be protected," according to the Holocaust Museum.

On the second day of the Battle of the Bulge, the Germans were winning and moving full speed ahead in their counteroffensive. On that day, December 17, 1944, from 80 to 130 American soldiers surrendered to the SS as prisoners of war. They were herded into the middle of the field, where they were systematically shot.

One survivor, Ted Paluch, described the massacre in a 2009 interview for Oral History Spotlight in the *News of the World War II Museum:*

> *One of the vehicles came around the corner and started firing into our group. I don't know who the hell it was,*

or why they started firing but they did. We were standing there with our hands up, and I was in the front of the group nearest the crossroads. As the German tank passed, they fired into the middle of us, everybody started to drop and I dropped too. I got hit in the hand as I went down. After that as each vehicle passed they fired into the group of us laying there dead or dying in the field. Anyone that was moaning they came around and finished them off. After that they went back and took off.

After laying there for I guess an hour or more I heard a voice I recognized yell, "Let's go!" so I got up and ran down a little road towards a hedgerow. The Germans came out of the house in the corner and took a shot at me and I dove into a hedgerow. I had some blood on me and I lay down in the hedgerow. I heard one of them running towards where I was lying and look me over, I could feel that guy standing above me, he could have shot me in the back and gotten it over with, but didn't. I knew he was waiting for me to move but I just laid there . . . dead still.[32]

Eventually he raised his head and when he saw no one, Paluch crawled along a railroad line into Malmedy where he ran into other survivors from his unit. After being interviewed by Army Intelligence, he went back to his unit for the rest of the war.

Dachau was a Nazi concentration camp first established in 1933 about 10 miles northwest of Munich in the state of Bavaria. It became a prototype for other camps and a training camp for the vicious SS guards. It was used for war crimes trials of lesser Nazis, including 70-plus tried for crimes related to Malmedy. Forty-three death sentences were issued related to Malmedy, but none was carried out. Thirty others were given lesser sentences.

In that same interview, Paluch said, "I don't know if we would have done that, but I don't really hold any animosity against them. I wish it didn't happen, but it did. A soldier gets orders just like we do and you carry them out. It's a hell of a thing, but it's war."

He also said he lost a lot of good friends who died that day. "I'm lucky . . . all my friends . . . all those young guys, they were all my age, with their whole life ahead of them. It never should have happened, and I hope no one ever forgets that it did."

Many times executions were changed to life in prison, although we did not knew that at the time. I was sorry to learn that the SS officers who had been convicted in the Malmedy Massacre escaped.

I cannot say that our soldiers never killed a POW—I have heard reports that some soldiers took revenge after hearing about Malmedy. It is never acceptable, and certainly our government would never condone such cold-blooded actions.

I Enter the Pipeline

> *26 August to 1 September 1945*
>
> Routine events. Getting ready to turn over the hospitals, but very busy now. 50 hospitals and 11 companies. Headquarters alerted on 1st of September for home. Morale sinks as we will be transferred out.

Arranging for the ambulances to take seven officers to Stuttgart, Germany, for executions was my last official act with my battalion. "Not much news, "I wrote in my Diary on November 6, 1945. "Sending out a few ambulances. Braddock and Boylan to haul seven SS War criminals to Stuttgart to be hung. Cannot shoot as that is an honorable death. One of them was officer responsible for shooting our POWs at Malmedy, Belgium."

> *11 August to 14 August 1945*
>
> Routine duties. Sweating out Jap surrender news. Started inspection trips to companies.
>
> *15 August 1945*
>
> Jap surrender announced. Listen to radio most of the day. Wonderful news.

I was assigned to the 522 Field Artillery Battalion with the expectation of leaving for France on November 9, only to learn on November 8 that my alert date was cancelled. I was assigned to be part of the 442nd Regimental Combat Team, which originally was composed of Japanese-American soldiers, mostly from the West Coast and Hawaii. These patriots chose to fight for their country, despite their family and friends being interred in U.S. camps "as enemy aliens," even if born in the United States. Men could leave these camps by volunteering for the Army, which Daniel Inouye did shortly after Pearl Harbor. He went on to earn the Medal of Honor, lost his arm in battle, and served as a U.S. Senator from Hawaii from 1959 until his death in 2012.

> *7 November 1945*
>
> This is it. Received news of my transfer to 522nd Field Artillery Battalion in Donaworth. They are alerted to go home and scheduled to leave for France 9 November. Packed and got affairs in order all day. Started saying good-bye.

During the war, we had very little news of what was going on anywhere else, and it was even limited in our immediate vicinity. I heard that Japanese-American soldiers, who mostly were from Hawaii and the West Coast, had fought in Italy but knew little about their service.

I since learned that units like the 522nd served distinctively in battles in Italy and in Germany, even helping to liberate some of the subcamps of the Dachau system. Scouts from this unit may even have arrived a day before other American units. Technician Fourth Grade Ichiro Imamura described the liberation in his diary that was quoted in Pierre Mulin's book, *Dachau, Holocaust and U.S. Samurais:*

> *I watched as one of the scouts used his carbine to shoot off the chain that held the prison gates shut. . . . They*

> *weren't dead, as he had first thought. When the gates swung open, we got our first good look at the prisoners. Many of them were Jews. They were wearing striped prison suits and round caps. It was cold and the snow was two feet deep in some places. There were no German guards. The prisoners struggled to their feet. . . . They shuffled weakly out of the compound. They were like skeletons—all skin and bones.*[33]

President Harry Truman greeted these returning Japanese-American soldiers in 1946 with the message, "You fought not only the enemy, but you fought prejudice, and you have won."[34]

Growing up in Marshall, Minnesota, we didn't have much diversity, as it is called today. Not only did I not meet an African American until I went to Minneapolis, I had never met anyone of Japanese descent. Once I was assigned to that unit for Japanese-American men to help process them home, I met 12 to 15 of the original soldiers. We worked together to process the papers to get the men of this unit—which now included many others—home as quickly as possible. I found them highly-educated, hardworking, bright men. They were the cream of the Army crop, the finest bunch of people I had ever worked with. They made my job easy.

We were together for several weeks and were choking in paper as these troops came in for processing. We had multiple changes in orders and delays before it was our turn to get moving ourselves.

Finally, we began moving on November 28. I woke at 2:30 a.m. to eat breakfast. We lined up in a convoy and departed at 5:20 a.m. on old 40 & 8 railroad cars, which were very uncomfortable boxcars without seats or padding. We were packed in like cattle on this train, which stopped periodically to allow us to get out and relieve ourselves.

These train cars were named 40 & 8 because they held either 40 soldiers or 8 horses during the First World War. With the U.S. needing to send millions of soldiers home, the Army turned many kinds of train cars into troop trains.

It was cold in early December 1945, so cold that one poor GI tried to start a fire to get warmth in the middle of a car packed with people. As the senior noncom on the train, I was responsible for this man. It was difficult to get him and the fire under control.

As terrible as the conditions were, we didn't complain, because we were heading away from war toward home. We traveled through Germany, then crossed into France at Metz, and finally stopped at Camp Chicago near Rheims, France. This redeployment camp, dubbed a "repo-depo," was one of many named for U.S. cities. It was a pretty good camp with PXes and theaters, but fuel was in short supply. Also, we lived in tents.

Finally we loaded trucks at 9 p.m. on December 16 and moved to the LeHavre Port of Embarkation. It was a very cold night, but we got coffee and donuts from the Red Cross.

Once we were at LaHavre, our wait was not over. We waited for a few days to be assigned to a ship and then for the ship to be ready for us. Lo and behold I ran into Fred—out of nine-million soldiers in Europe eager to get home—and discovered we had been assigned to the same ship, the Sheepshead Bay Victory Ship. We could not believe our good luck to be together again. While we waited a few days for the ship, we sampled the various opportunities at Camp Chicago, including booths of French women who worked from a variety of stands selling refreshments and services like trimming nails and hair.

Fred and I were separated during the occupation—the first time since boot camp. Since he was a college graduate who had taught high school chemistry, physics, and math for a year before entering the Army, he was assigned to teach science courses to GIs at a small German college taken over by the U.S. Army. Fred taught physics to men who otherwise would have little to do but wait.

I was able to get a jeep to visit Fred a couple times during the occupation. Since he was an only child, I think he looked at me as a brother he never had. We had no idea when we would see each other again, but of course promised to get together in the United States.

The Sheepshead Bay was a nice, clean little ship, but we were packed in on layers of bunks. With storms on the North Atlantic the captain decided to take a southern course via the Azores. As I wrote in my diary, "Channel very rough and everyone starts getting sick in evening. Really a mess."

I was sick on the second and third day along with three-fourths of the 1,550 troops, 20 civilians and eight Red Cross workers on the ship. One day, the ship captain told us that we had only moved 22 nautical miles forward in the previous 24 hours, but probably traveled a thousand miles up and down. It was that bad, so bad at times we were afraid we *wouldn't* die.

We bounced around much more on that little ship than we would have in a larger vessel. Most of us just stayed in our bunks, trying to keep anything down we could—even if just crackers. The first day that I actually made it down to the mess hall, I sat at a table with three or four other guys. Another soldier came and sat right across from me, immediately throwing up all over his tray and mine. It didn't do much for my stomach, still in precarious shape. Rather than getting another tray, I headed back to my bunk and just ate more crackers.

When we were up to it, we talked in the mess about our experiences in the war. One tank driver—the commanding noncom of his three-man tank crew—told me about his unit's transfer from the 7th Army to Patton's 3rd Army. They were in Northern France and had the objective of retaking the Maginot Line. General Patton came to inspect the new unit as part of the reassignment from the 7th, which he earlier had led into Sicily, Italy. Patton lost that command after he slapped two men in an evacuation hospital in the battle for Sicily.

When Patton arrived in the hospital unexpectedly, he demanded to know, "What's wrong with these soldiers?" He called them cowards and slapped them.

He later was forced to apologize to all the men in front

of him and lost his leadership role for a time. General Omar Bradley became the general responsible for the overall invasion of Normandy and Lt. General Mark Clark was assigned to lead the 7th Army.

Historic reports indicate that Patton, whom the Nazis reportedly feared, was supposed to be in Dover, England, during much of 1944. That diversion was part of a massive misinformation plan designed to convince the Nazis the Allies would land at Pas de Calais, France. Germany took the bite, sending its 15th Army there to defend against what it figured would be a massive invasion led by Patton. Meanwhile, the general was actually training with the 3rd Army for the battle in Normandy.

Each tank crew stood in front of its tank for Patton's inspection on the day of transfer. As Generals Clark and Patton approached, the sergeant who was in the first tank to be inspected overheard a heated conversation between the two generals.

"Who the hell authorized these tanks to be sandbagged?" Patton demanded to know.

"I did, sir, because it saves a lot of casualties."

"No sandbagging in the 3rd Army."

Sandbags were tied to any flat surface on tanks to absorb shrapnel from shells and other weapons. Patton ordered them all removed so the tanks moved faster.

Patton stuck his face up into the face of the man who told me this story. "What's the matter, soldier? Are you afraid to die?"

"You're damn right I am, sir," he responded with a sharp salute.

The sergeant said he did not know if Patton would shoot him with one of the revolvers he carried or discipline him in some way. Instead, the general moved on to the next tank.

I also heard the story of another soldier whose was assigned to take a hill in Northern France, where the Germans were dug in and shooting down on the American soldiers. Casualties mounted, their unit was becoming depleted, and they struggled to keep rifles on the line. The regimental commander asked permission to withdraw until they could get reinforcements for the lost men. That request went up the chain of command with permission given by each officer until it reached Patton.

Patton, according to the story that infantry regiment sergeant told me at the 109th Evacuation Hospital, was not sympathetic. "I want that damn hill even if it takes a truckload of dog tags to get it," Patton said. "Keep those men on the line."

They finally got up that damn hill, but their unit had 80-percent casualties —in men killed or wounded. No wonder the men made fun of the "Old Blood and Guts" nickname for Patton. "Our blood," many men said, "and his guts."

Nearly to New York

Conditions on board our ship improved the last day or two as we neared New York. We celebrated Christmas on board and then landed the day after.

As the senior noncom on the ship, I worked closely with Army officers, making announcements when needed, as well as handling paperwork and other assignments. It was important to know if any of us were sick beyond seasickness before we left the ship so arrangements could be made for their care.

18 December to 28 December 1945 (Final Entry)

At sea. Long, slow, rough going. I was sick 2nd and 3rd day, but got over it. Three-fourths of boat violently sick first few days. Start working for Lt. Orr and Transport Service. Good deal. Worked on Christmas issue of paper. Very good Christmas dinner considering the circumstances. 1550 troops, 20 civilians, and 8 Red Cross girls on board. Fred's outfit also on board. Much disease develops—scabies, VD, etc. Really anxious to hit land. Due in NY 29 December 1945.

CHAPTER SIX

Returning to Civilian Life

When you've been gone from the United States for any reason, but especially for war, there is nothing better than seeing the Statue of Liberty as you approach the United States. In our case, it was right after Christmas when we came into the port of New York at night. It was a thrill, just wonderful to see the lights of Lady Liberty again after years of blackout during the war.

We took a train into New York and then another to Fort Dix, New Jersey, where we did our initial processing. We were on such a high to be back that it felt like our feet only touched the ground every third step or so. But we were also exhausted and hungry. They fed us big steak dinners served by German Prisoners of War. A GI in front of me was not pleased with the size steak he was given. "Listen, dammit! I fought you for three years and I want a big steak." The eager-to-oblige POW brought him two more.

We spent a few days at a camp in New Jersey before going by train to various locations in the country to process our actual discharges. We Midwesterners went to Camp McCoy, Wisconsin, which is located in western Wisconsin, about three hours from Minneapolis.

I probably sent my parents a telegram—the text message

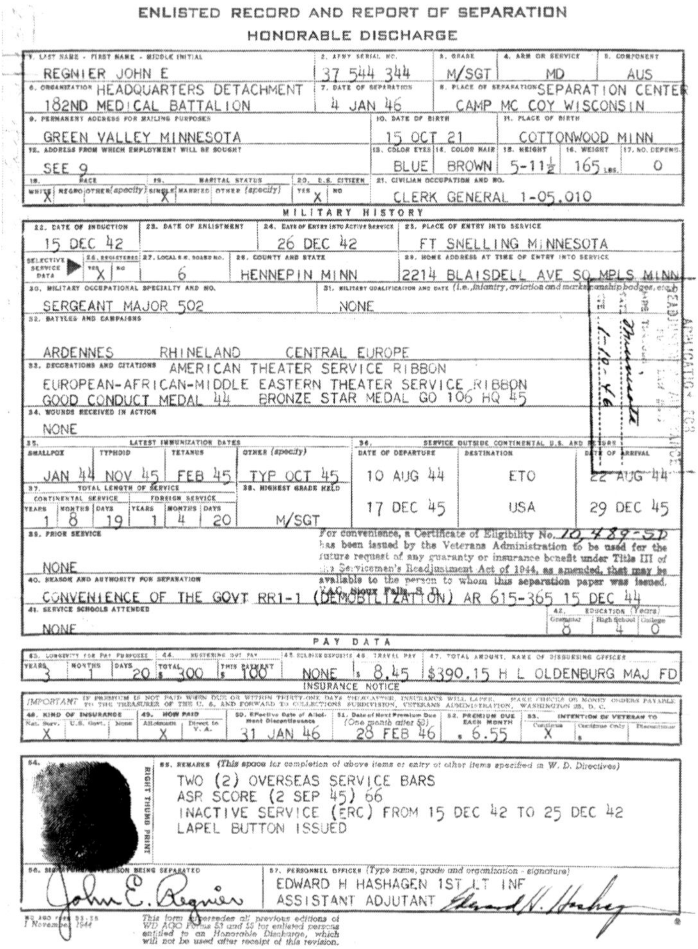

ENLISTED RECORD AND REPORT OF SEPARATION
HONORABLE DISCHARGE

1. LAST NAME - FIRST NAME - MIDDLE INITIAL: REGNIER JOHN E
2. ARMY SERIAL NO.: 37 544 344
3. GRADE: M/SGT
4. ARM OR SERVICE: MD
5. COMPONENT: AUS
6. ORGANIZATION: HEADQUARTERS DETACHMENT 182ND MEDICAL BATTALION
7. DATE OF SEPARATION: 4 JAN 46
8. PLACE OF SEPARATION: SEPARATION CENTER CAMP MC COY WISCONSIN
9. PERMANENT ADDRESS FOR MAILING PURPOSES: GREEN VALLEY MINNESOTA
10. DATE OF BIRTH: 15 OCT 21
11. PLACE OF BIRTH: COTTONWOOD MINN
12. ADDRESS FROM WHICH EMPLOYMENT WILL BE SOUGHT: SEE 9
13. COLOR EYES: BLUE
14. COLOR HAIR: BROWN
15. HEIGHT: 5-11½
16. WEIGHT: 165 LBS.
17. NO. DEPEND.: 0
18. RACE: WHITE X — NEGRO — OTHER (specify)
19. MARITAL STATUS: SINGLE X — MARRIED — OTHER (specify)
20. U.S. CITIZEN: YES X — NO
21. CIVILIAN OCCUPATION AND NO.: CLERK GENERAL 1-05.010

MILITARY HISTORY

22. DATE OF INDUCTION: 15 DEC 42
23. DATE OF ENLISTMENT:
24. DATE OF ENTRY INTO ACTIVE SERVICE: 26 DEC 42
25. PLACE OF ENTRY INTO SERVICE: FT SNELLING MINNESOTA
SELECTIVE SERVICE DATA — 26. REGISTERED: YES X — NO
27. LOCAL S.S. BOARD NO.: 6
28. COUNTY AND STATE: HENNEPIN MINN
29. HOME ADDRESS AT TIME OF ENTRY INTO SERVICE: 2214 BLAISDELL AVE SO MPLS MINN
30. MILITARY OCCUPATIONAL SPECIALTY AND NO.: SERGEANT MAJOR 502
31. MILITARY QUALIFICATION AND DATE (i.e., infantry, aviation and marksmanship badges, etc.): NONE
32. BATTLES AND CAMPAIGNS: ARDENNES RHINELAND CENTRAL EUROPE
33. DECORATIONS AND CITATIONS: AMERICAN THEATER SERVICE RIBBON EUROPEAN-AFRICAN-MIDDLE EASTERN THEATER SERVICE RIBBON GOOD CONDUCT MEDAL 44 BRONZE STAR MEDAL GO 106 HQ 45
34. WOUNDS RECEIVED IN ACTION: NONE

35. LATEST IMMUNIZATION DATES

SMALLPOX	TYPHOID	TETANUS	OTHER (specify)
JAN 44	NOV 45	FEB 45	TYP OCT 45

36. SERVICE OUTSIDE CONTINENTAL U.S. AND RETURN

DATE OF DEPARTURE	DESTINATION	DATE OF ARRIVAL
10 AUG 44	ETO	22 AUG 44
17 DEC 45	USA	29 DEC 45

37. TOTAL LENGTH OF SERVICE

Continental Service Years	Months	Days	Foreign Service Years	Months	Days
1	8	19	1	4	20

38. HIGHEST GRADE HELD: M/SGT
39. PRIOR SERVICE: NONE

For convenience, a Certificate of Eligibility No. 10,489-SD has been issued by the Veterans Administration to be used for the future request of any guaranty or insurance benefit under Title III of the Servicemen's Readjustment Act of 1944, as amended, that may be available to the person to whom this separation paper was issued. VAC, Sioux Falls, S. D.

40. REASON AND AUTHORITY FOR SEPARATION: CONVENIENCE OF THE GOVT RR1-1 (DEMOBILIZATION) AR 615-365 15 DEC 44
41. SERVICE SCHOOLS ATTENDED: NONE
42. EDUCATION (Years): Grammar 8 — High School 4 — College 0

PAY DATA

43. Longevity for Pay Purposes Years	Months	Days	44. Mustering Out Pay Total	This Payment	45. Soldiers Deposits	46. Travel Pay	47. Total Amount, Name of Disbursing Officer
3	1	20	$ 300	$ 100	NONE	$ 8.45	$390.15 H L OLDENBURG MAJ FD

INSURANCE NOTICE

IMPORTANT IF PREMIUM IS NOT PAID WHEN DUE OR WITHIN THIRTY-ONE DAYS THEREAFTER, INSURANCE WILL LAPSE. MAKE CHECKS OR MONEY ORDERS PAYABLE TO THE TREASURER OF THE U. S. AND FORWARD TO COLLECTIONS SUBDIVISION, VETERANS ADMINISTRATION, WASHINGTON 25, D. C.

48. Kind of Insurance	49. How Paid	50. Effective Date of Allotment Discontinuance	51. Date of Next Premium Due (One month after 50)	52. Premium Due Each Month	53. Intention of Veteran To
Nat. Serv. X	Allotment X	31 JAN 46	28 FEB 46	$ 6.55	Continue X

54. RIGHT THUMB PRINT

55. REMARKS (This space for completion of above items or entry of other items specified in W. D. Directives)
TWO (2) OVERSEAS SERVICE BARS
ASR SCORE (2 SEP 45) 66
INACTIVE SERVICE (ERC) FROM 15 DEC 42 TO 25 DEC 42
LAPEL BUTTON ISSUED

56. SIGNATURE OF PERSON BEING SEPARATED: John E. Regnier
57. PERSONNEL OFFICER (Type name, grade and organization - signature): EDWARD H HASHAGEN 1ST LT INF ASSISTANT ADJUTANT Edward H. Hashagen

WD AGO Form 53-55, 1 November 1944
This form supersedes all previous editions of WD AGO Forms 53 and 55 for enlisted persons entitled to an Honorable Discharge, which will not be used after receipt of this revision.

The document for my honorable discharge.

of the day—to tell them I was back in the country and would see them soon. You didn't telephone long distance in those days as it was too expensive.

At Camp McCoy, I received my final pay—I had not gotten any for the last three months so I had a pretty good check coming. Camp officials also provided information about The Servicemen's Readjustment Act of 1944, commonly known as the GI Bill. Although it was controversial, Congress passed the law to prevent the problems that arose after World War I when returning soldiers were just given $60 and a train ticket home.

Many Doughboys, as they were called in World War I, found it hard to get jobs and to adjust to civilian life, and were especially hurt during the Great Depression. Conditions were so bad that they marched on Washington in 1932 demanding full payment of the bonuses they were to receive based on the number of days served. That bonus was not supposed to be paid for 20 years after service, and these vets were hungry right then.[35]

In signing the GI bill on June 22, 1944, President Roosevelt described it as:

- Giving Servicemen and women the opportunity to resume their education or technical training after discharge, or of taking a refresher or retraining course, not only without tuition up to $500 per school year, but with the right to receive a monthly living allowance while pursuing their studies.

- Providing for the guarantee by the Federal Government of not to exceed 50 percent of certain loans made to veterans for the purchase or construction of homes, farms, and business properties.
- Providing for reasonable unemployment allowances payable each week up to a maximum period of one year, to those veterans who are unable to find a job.
- Improving machinery for effective job counseling for veterans and for finding jobs for returning soldiers and sailors.
- Authorizing the construction of all necessary additional hospital facilities.
- Strengthening the authority of the Veterans Administration to enable it to discharge its existing and added responsibilities with promptness and efficiency.

In a fireside chat on July 28, 1943, President Roosevelt said, "Among many other things we are, today, laying plans for the return to civilian life of our gallant men and women in the armed services. They must not be demobilized into an environment of inflation and unemployment, to a place on a bread line, or on a corner selling apples. We must, this time, have plans ready, instead of waiting to do a hasty, inefficient, and ill-considered job at the last moment."

This bill, dubbed the "Magic Carpet to the Middle Class,"

was considered to be the most important legislation in the 20th Century. It built the middle class by helping millions attend college by providing tuition, fee and books, plus $65-a-month in living expenses. Soldiers who did not want to go to college instead received living expenses for up to 52 weeks, a benefit that ended when they found a job. The government found a tremendous recouping of its spending through this program. For every dollar spent on a veteran's education, local economics received many more dollars in return as these vets had better jobs with higher incomes. Not only could they buy more, which stimulated the economy, they also paid more into the tax system, which helped pay for the program.

I could not wait to get going on my education, catching a ride with a few other Minnesota GIs in a car that someone had. I wanted to stop in St. Paul before heading to Marshall to see Uncle Hank and Aunt Marc and, even more important, to find out if I could enter the University of Minnesota right away. The university was then on the quarter system, which meant classes had already begun. Admissions staff suggested I enroll that semester in a college that had not yet started classes. I could transfer back to the university in the fall.

I was still in my uniform when I signed up classes at the College of St. Thomas. Then, wanting to get civilian clothes before heading to Marshall, I stopped at stores on Washington Avenue in Minneapolis to find a suit. Men's clothes were almost impossible to find because little had been made during the Great Depression, and then during the war most young men were in uniform. I finally found a small store with a suit, but the pants were way too large for me. The owner said he could alter them, and when he did, the pockets were so close to each other that I could reach both pockets with one hand. Needless to say, I only wore it home that one time.

It was wonderful to reunite with my parents and siblings. I was not the only Regnier in the military during World War II. My oldest brother, Bill, went in the Army about 18 months before I did. After training in a field artillery battalion in California, his first assignment was in Africa towards the end of the war there. He then moved on from Africa to Sicily, Italy. In the field artillery unit, he was safer than being at the front lines, although those of us who were in support roles were in even less peril.

When my brother, Jim, reported for his Army physical, he was rejected because of a heart murmur. Although he had Rheumatic Fever as a child, he had no idea that he had this mild murmur. Disappointed he could not fight in the war, he worked in a defense plant. I'm sure it was tough on him not to be in uniform, as young men were looked on as slackers if they were not in the military.

By the time my younger brother, Wally, graduated from high school, the draft age had dropped to 18. Thus, he was 1A immediately after graduation. After infantry training in California, he was shipped to New Guinea, where preparation was being made to retake The Philippines from the Japanese. He was in on terrible fighting, landing first on the beach on the

This photo may be the only that shows our entire family together. *From left:* Bobby, Bill, Irene, Doris, Dick, Dean, Jim, me, Mother, Betts, Father, and Wally.

I'm shown here with my family in about 1948 or 1949. *From left:* me, Dick, Dean, Bill, Mom, Wally, Jim, and Bobby.

east side of the jungle area. Part of the U.S. strategy was taking the lesser-populated parts of The Philippines on the way to Manila. The Japanese dug in tremendously, unwilling to give up what they had taken away from the U.S. earlier in the war. After we reunited in Marshall, I learned more about Wally's experiences. The terrible fighting was on the beach and then in the jungle with extreme heat and beastly insects. Each night Wally and another GI took turns digging a foxhole and guarding. The task was difficult because there were many underground crossing roots.

My brother stood up from the digging to rest for a moment. Just as he bent back over to dig again, a Japanese sniper hiding in a tree fired. That movement saved Wally—the bullet just went in and out of flesh on his back—instead of hitting him in his unprotected head. Wally didn't wear his helmet because it was so beastly hot. His partner immediately spotted where the shot came from and killed the sniper immediately.

This story shows how quickly life and death decisions were made during the war. A split-second made the difference between Wally living and dying. If he hadn't moved the second he did, he would have died.

Wally went back to the medical station, where he received a few stitches and was returned to duty, which involved still more days of fierce fighting on the beach. The Japanese had time before the U.S. Army arrived to dig in, which made the fighting so miserable. The Japanese also bombarded the area with artillery and fighter planes.

About two or weeks later, after they had moved into the jungle, it was Wally's turn to catch a few hours of sleep while his partner stood guard. An artillery shell hit the foxhole next to them, killing the men inside it. The concussion nearly blew Wally's head off, and he was thrown up into the air eight to ten feet, knocking him unconscious when he landed. A corpsman evacuated Wally, who was in shock and had a ruptured eardrum, to a hospital ship in the harbor. He and other men unable to recover enough to return to duty were sent back to the United States. Wally recovered in a military hospital in Michigan.

After his discharge from the hospital, Wally expected to go to college, but the day after he came home, he stopped by Western State Bank in Marshall to set up an account for the money he had not spent over the previous three months. When the bank president, who had run the bank since her husband died, heard the name Regnier she came out of her office to welcome Wally home. After visiting with him, she asked what he planned to do. He told her he planned to rest up before going to school. She offered him a job as a teller, which he started a few days later. Wally stayed his entire career there, moving up to executive vice president, the second highest position in the bank.

Dean, who was not old enough to serve during World War II, served in the signal corps in Germany during the Korean War. My brother Dick was in the Air Corps, serving in Guam during Korea.

Jim, who had the heart condition that prevented him from serving during World War II, ended up with an outstanding career as CEO of Blue Cross/Blue Shield of Minnesota, while my brother Bob became an English professor at St. Cloud State University in Minnesota.

My Plans

After spending time with my family in Marshall, Minnesota, I was eager to get on with my life. I used the education benefit for a year as an undergraduate student first at St. Thomas for a semester with the hope of transferring to the University of Minnesota. But with so many men coming home from the war, the pre-medicine program was filled. I instead transferred to St. Cloud State University for the year, again under the GI Bill. With my original intention of going to medical school, I decided to defer the rest of my education benefit because I figured medical school would be so much more expensive than undergraduate studies.

During my years at the university, I worked summers for the Minnesota Department of Agriculture, where my Uncle Hank was head of the certified seed potato inspector unit. Uncle Hank, who like my father had only attended school through the eighth grade, was a self-educated man who worked and competed successfully with many college graduates, even those who held PhDs. Uncle Hank rose to be head of his department.

My job was to visit farms in Northern Minnesota to inspect their potato seed programs. Buying certified seed was important because it helped ensure crops would be disease free, or at least more likely to be disease free. This work was very important, as the success of farmers across the state of Minnesota depended on the quality of the seeds they planted.

Meeting Eva Mae

I went home to Marshall a few days before I was to graduate from the University of Minnesota with my degree in 3-1/2 years. Wally, who was working at the bank, ran into a schoolteacher in Marshall each morning at the post office. Knowing I was coming home for the weekend, he asked Eva Mae Cann if she was going to the dance at the Blue Moon Ballroom Friday night. Wally was asking for me—not that I knew it at the time—because he was in a relationship with a woman he later married. Eva Mae had hoped Wally was asking for himself, but agreed to meet me when I came in town.

Eva Mae actually taught my two youngest brothers, Dick and Dean. She was exactly the kind of woman I hoped to meet—smart, good-looking, with a wonderful sense of humor. We had a wonderful time at the dance and then began to see each other whenever I came to Marshall. We had time to get to know each other as I spent a little longer time in town that summer before I started my summer job in late June.

Eva Mae grew up in Blackduck, Minnesota, and graduated with a teaching degree from Bemidji State University. After teaching in schools in and around Blackduck for a couple years, she decided to accept a position in Marshall.

After a year or two in Marshall, Eva Mae resigned her position, thinking she wanted to do something different, possibly a Lutheran missionary program. Her family had moved to St. Paul as her father, Harry Cann, had taken a job as chief game warden for the state of Minnesota. He had been a wonderful game warden because he loved the outdoors, but was not happy as the chief because he spent too much time behind the desk. Eva Mae's mother Lydia (Sorenson) had not yet joined her husband in St. Paul.

Eva Mae and I decided we were serious about each other fairly quickly. Although we had not set a date for marriage, I had talked with a cousin, Warren Regnier, a newly-ordained priest, about officiating when we did get married. As assistant pastor at St. Philip's Church in Bemidji, Minnesota, in the summer of 1949, he offered to marry us if we wanted to come to Bemidji for the ceremony. I saw him frequently because I was inspecting seed-potato seeds in that area.

Our ceremony ended up in East Grand Forks, Minnesota, on June 24, 1950, because my cousin had transferred there to be the assistant priest at Sacred Heart Church. It was a very small ceremony—almost as if we had eloped. Because of the distance, not that many family members came to the celebration.

Our wedding occurred during a downpour, which distracted my attention momentarily as I wondered whether I had rolled up the windows in our car. As a result, I did not rise from the kneeling position at the cue the priest gave us earlier for when we should come forward. Eva Mae loved to tease me about not being the best romantic on our wedding day.

Eva Mae and I were very happy on our wedding day.

We spent our honeymoon at Rustic Rest in Detroit Lakes, Minnesota.

Although it was a small ceremony, our marriage lasted 63 years until Eva Mae's death in 2012. We were wonderful partners, supporting each other through good and bad times.

In 1950, after Eva Mae and I were married, I worked my third and last year with the Minnesota Department of Agriculture. At that point, I was a supervisor, and we were based in Moorhead, Minnesota, where Eva Mae took some courses toward her graduate degree, which she later finished at age 50 after our last child started school.

Before I started that job, we had a week-long honeymoon in a little cabin at Detroit Lakes, a popular tourist area just east of Moorhead. It was a wonderful time, although the day after our wedding I was upset upon hearing the news about the start of the Korean War. I reacted so strongly that I'm sure Eva Mae wondered what sort of man she had married. I found that news so disturbing because I felt I had just gotten home from one war and I hadn't made real inroads into starting a career and having a family.

Each morning that week we went into Detroit Lakes for Mass and shopping. One day, we decided to do some fishing on this beautiful clear-water lake. Since we didn't have equipment with us, we borrowed a boat and gear from the lady who owned the tourist cabins. It was a beautiful day with wonderful weather, but somehow the minnow bucket came loose and fell to the bottom of the lake at the sandy bottom. We knew we had to get that bucket back, but I did not swim. Eva Mae did, so we decided she would dive for it. When she couldn't get deep enough to reach the bucket, she suggested we go back to shore and borrow a bamboo pole to reach down eight to ten feet below.

But how would we ever find our way back to that exact spot? She saw two landmarks on the shore that she zeroed in on creating a geometric image in her mind. We hoped we didn't see our landlady when we went back for the pole. The soaking-wet Eva Mae joked the woman probably thought, "One day of marriage, and already he's trying to drown her."

We put a hook on the end of the end of the longest bamboo pole I could find and then headed back to the middle of the lake, where Eva Mae used her geometric pattern to triangulate the spot where the bucket would be. There it was, and up it came with the pole.

On our second night as Eva Mae was fixing us dinner, she looked all over for a cutting board, but none was found. We asked the landlady if she had one, but she did not. I then volunteered to make cutting boards for her and each of the cabins if she provided me with plywood and tools. It was a fair exchange.

After that wonderful week, I was off to inspect potatoes in Moorhead. Housing after the millions of soldiers came home after World War II was terribly tight, as little construction was done during the years of the Great Depression or during the war. At first all I could find in Moorhead was the basement—unfinished—in the home of two old, unmarried sisters named LaVeet. It was clean, but left a lot to be desired. I asked and they agreed to allow me to put cardboard over our bed and table as a kind of ceiling. They were very sweet ladies who welcomed the company, even offered Eva Mae the rainwater they collected for washing her hair.

After a couple of weeks, I was happy to find a cabin where we had more space and privacy. It came with a small refrigerator and a sink with a washing machine. Its location three miles outside of Moorhead meant I dropped Eva Mae in town each day so she could attend more classes at Moorhead State University while I worked.

Meanwhile, I needed to figure out what to do with my career. I had good grades and applied for medical school at the University of Minnesota after my junior and senior years of college, but didn't quite make the cut from the final selection rounds. With so many million men coming out of the military at the same time, there simply were not enough slots available for those like myself who would be good candidates at any other time. At the time, the Medical School only took 110 students a year and there were 2,100 applicants the first year and 2,800 the second. The problem was that we were all finishing undergraduate school at about the same time after the war.

Soldiers who were able to get out of the army sooner and started college before me were able to apply in years that were not as competitive, especially if they had finished a year or two of college before the war. I never begrudged their acceptances into medical school.

The intense competition in those years was confirmed to me when I paced back and forth in the father's waiting room at

Mount Sinai Hospital in Minneapolis, waiting for the birth of our son Greg. The assistant dean of the medical school, who also was waiting for his child to be born, was quite interested in my experience in pre-med.

When he heard it, the dean shook his head. Things had changed so much by then that they were only getting three or four applicants for each position. He told me I would have no problem getting in if I wanted to apply then, but I had started another career and was happy with it.

After I didn't get in that second year, I considered a course in hospital administration, but I decided instead to use the last of my GI Bill for courses that would qualify me to teach. I earned that teaching degree from St. Cloud State University in 1951, while Eva Mae taught in the Anoka, Minnesota, School District.

Housing still was very difficult to find after the war, with many of us coming back wanting to start families or already having families. For that first year, we stayed in a hotel in Anoka in what was little more than a room, a bathroom, and a small kitchen area.

Shortly after I finished that teaching program, I helped my brother-in-law Hugh trim a hedge at their St. Louis Park home. He had been in a surgical residency when war began. After spending the war years on a hospital ship in the Pacific, he returned to Minnesota, where he re-entered his surgical residency. In the midst of that training, Dr. Ruth Boynton, the first female head of a university health service in the country, offered Hugh a position with the University of Minnesota health service. She knew the importance of the program, because as an undergraduate student, she had barely survived the 1918 influenza pandemic that turned the student union into a makeshift hospital.[36] Hugh left the residency and took the position, which he enjoyed for the rest of his career.

As I left Hugh's house, getting a teaching job was foremost on my mind. When I happened by the St. Louis Park High School, I decided to stop there to pick up an application for the school year. It was late in the afternoon on a summer day, but the woman in the office said the principal was there if I had time to speak with him. We talked for about a half hour, and then he brought in the superintendent to speak with me. They then conferred for a few minutes and said they were pretty sure they could offer me a job. I filled out an application and arranged for my transcripts to be sent from both the University of Minnesota and St. Cloud State University.

The next day, I signed a contract to teach sophomore World History classes and one class of Social Problems for seniors. I never worked so hard in my life as I did that year at St. Louis Park High School. The students were terrific, as were the staff. Ten to twelve boys frequently visited me after class, wanting to hear my stories about the war. I think the students appreciated me because I had so many real-life experiences from the war to share in world history lessons.

The year went well, but I decided I would not be satisfied long-term with the economics of teaching if I wanted to raise a family. That summer, I told Eva Mae that I wanted to look for a job in business. I felt I would have more control and more opportunities in business than in education. She agreed.

Meanwhile, Eva Mae and I now lived in a four-plex apartment building. We furnished it with money I had saved from my time in the service. All those many months in Europe, I had nothing to spend my pay on so I sent it home in the form of war bonds. That money provided us with an opportunity to buy our furniture and appliances from Sears.

During the summer of 1951 after that year of teaching, we went to Midland, Michigan, traveling in our first new car, a Plymouth, that we bought for $1,700. I had loved our first car, a 1939 Chevy Touring Sedan, which we traded in for $400.

Our plan was to drive to Manitowoc, Wisconsin, and then take the ferry across Lake Michigan to visit Aunt Sis (Adeline), my dad's youngest sister, and Uncle Earl LaBeau. Uncle Earl owned his own jewelry store in Midland, Michigan.

On the way there, we drove through Stevens Point, Wisconsin, where we saw a large building that was the home of Hardware Mutual Insurance. I didn't know much about insurance then, but this seemed like a promising company to learn more about for a possible career. Hardware Mutual, now Sentry Insurance, was founded in 1904 to serve the needs of the Wisconsin Retail Hardware Association, now the Midwest Hardware Association, offering life, group health, and other property and casualty lines for individuals, groups, and businesses across the country.

When I went back to Minnesota, I discovered a newspaper advertisement for a job with the Minnesota office of the company as a claims adjuster. I went to the district office and spoke with the personnel manager, who took my application. He told me that the company was expanding so rapidly that it used a psychological consultant to evaluate college graduates as prospective employees. This consultant would not be coming to Minneapolis for a few weeks, but if I wanted to speed things up I could go to Chicago for an appointment with Dr. Mack Henderson there.

I agreed to do so in the summer of 1952, but first went ahead with a planned visit with Fred and his family in Cedar Falls the weekend before. We knew I could still make my 10 a.m. appointment in Chicago that Monday.

I went through a battery of tests that day, but didn't get a report. We finished with time to spare before our 10 p.m. train back to Minneapolis, so we decided to explore Chicago.

This appointment coincided with the first day of the Republican Convention in 1952, where General Eisenhower and Robert A. Taft both sought the Republican nomination. General Douglas MacArthur—the general President Truman had fired for insubordination in 1951—was the keynote speaker. Truman advocated a limited war in Korea while MacArthur wanted to go all out.

This was a much different, more innocent time when security was not like it is today. Eva Mae and I walked through the Republican Headquarters at the Hilton Hotel without anyone questioning us. Growing up, I occasionally went to political rallies with my dad and uncle and had many political talks over dinner. I'd never seen this many Republicans in one place before.

Since we had the time, we decided to catch the speech in the hotel. Each of the candidates had a meeting room with seats set up to watch the convention. We picked the headquarters for Harold Stassen, Minnesota governor from 1939 to 1943, and who was a perennial Republican candidate for president, running nine times: 1948, 1952, 1956, 1960, 1964, 1968, 1972, 1976, and 1988. In 1952, he turned over his delegates to Eisenhower, which gave the former general the nomination on the first ballot.

On that night, there was plenty of room for us at the Stassen headquarters, where we observed people coming and going. Among them was a very wealthy-looking couple who came into the Stassen viewing site. We saw how this much-bejeweled woman ruled over her husband, who did whatever she demanded.

All of a sudden, the wife poked her husband and noted there was a "Negro" (the term used then) at the door. The man apparently knew he should not come in unless he was invited. She suggested her husband shake the man's hand because it "would look good." She didn't suggest inviting him in; she just wanted her husband to pretend to care about the man at the door. I was shocked that such a connection would be all about looking good, rather than sincerely wanting to meet and include him in the activities.

CHAPTER SEVEN

Sentry Career and Family Life

I received a job offer from Hardware Mutual in 1952, staying there 32 years until I retired in 1984 from what later became Sentry. For the first few months, I was in training as an insurance adjustor, who investigates claims to determine the company's liability. I liked this work, learning about every aspect of business from clients to working with high-end attorneys.

After training, I was assigned to a territory in Minneapolis, which I kept until I was promoted to resident claims adjustor based in Sioux Falls, South Dakota. My territory included eastern South Dakota, southwestern Minnesota, and northeastern Iowa. The company had promised the adjuster in Sioux Falls that he could transfer to Minneapolis so he could attend law school at night. We moved to Sioux Falls, where we found a little house that had two bedrooms, living room, kitchen, and a nice basement where I put my office, since I worked out of my home.

Our first child was born at Christmas 1952. Eva Mae taught kindergarten—subbing for a teacher who had become sick—up until about three weeks before Dougie was born. It was very unusual then—most pregnant women left the workforce when they began showing, but the district was that desperate for a kindergarten teacher. The hardest part of teaching for her was to get boots that were too small on the feet of her students. Eventually, she told the school principal that if they didn't want her to have the baby right in the classroom, she needed to leave.

All was going well for the first six months of Dougie's life. Then he began to have petit mal seizures, sometimes called absence seizures, with brief, sudden lapses of consciousness. We didn't know what was happening at first, and Dougie was a big, husky baby who started walking at 11 months.

Meanwhile, Dougie had grand mal seizures, which involve violent muscle contractions along with loss of consciousness. It was getting worse, and instead of developing he was losing ground. We went to see Dr. Lund, our pediatrician in St. Louis Park, Minnesota, a Minneapolis suburb. This doctor referred us to a pediatric neurologist, who said if they could control his seizures with new medications, he would develop normally.

With the seizures continuing, my brother-in-law Hugh suggested we take Dougie to see a medical school colleague of his, Dr. Brown, who was assistant dean of the neurology department at the University of Minnesota. This Dr. Brown did a very thorough exam, surprisingly zeroing in on a birthmark on his lower back on the belt line. We had known about the birthmark, but our pediatrician told us not to worry about unless it grows or changes abnormally.

Dr. Brown told us that if his theory is correct, there may be similar birthmarks on his brain or elsewhere in the body. It was not good news.

After being hospitalized for a few days for tests, the brain scan showed tuberous sclerosis, which causes non-malignant tumors to grow on the brain and other vital organs. Symptoms include seizures, developmental delay, behavioral problems, skin abnormalities, and lung and kidney diseases.

We learned surgery was not an option as it was too widespread. Dougie likely had a life expectancy of 12 to 14 years, and he would become more and more disabled physically and mentally.

Why did this happen? Dr. Brown said the most likely cause without a genetic family history was something went wrong in the very early development of the embryo. He told us that the previous doctors who had not been able to help identify the cause of the seizures were not wrong. Tuberous sclerosis was rarely known then; you almost had to be in a combination of a clinic and academic practice to make the diagnosis.

I went to the university medical school library to learn more about the condition, but could only find two books that mentioned it, and they were translated from a German textbook. This was a time when doctors urged families to place their children in a hospital for children with developmental disabilities.

However, we decided to join MARC (Minneapolis Association for Retarded Children), although Eva Mae was reluctant at first. She felt it was not going to help Dougie, but I thought learning more about his problem might help us. She agreed.

Surprisingly, we reconnected with a doctor there who had joined the group with his wife after their first child was born with a developmental disability. I knew him as an undergraduate student. One thing I learned was that having a child with a serious disability crossed every social, economic, racial, ethnic, and educational line. It could happen to any of us.

I was invited to serve on the MARC Board of Directors and met really wonderful people at the meetings. I was scheduled to be chair of the board when I was offered a position in Sentry's corporate office in Stevens Point, Wisconsin.

With John F. Kennedy in the White House, more attention was drawn to children with mental retardation, thanks to the work of Eunice Shriver, sister of President Kennedy. Her work lead to a national conference in Washington, D.C. My successor as chair at MARC went instead of me.

Eva Mae had the opportunity to speak to various groups about being a parent of a child with a developmental disability. I was tied up with work so I could not go with her when she was on a panel at the University of Minnesota. This concerned the person organizing the event, Don Omodt, then sheriff of Hennepin County. He told me he would sit by her to provide support.

The panel was given this question to begin: "What did your parents think when they learned you had a retarded child?" Eva Mae, bless her, said something like "My parents thought it had to be something on his side and his parents thought it had to be from my side."

That broke up the room. The organizer of the event leaned over to Eva Mae and whispered, "You don't need my help."

Our son, Greg, the second born and a couple of years younger than Dougie, was wonderful during the years his big brother was home with us. He kept an eye on Dougie in the yard, making sure he didn't harm himself. He loved that little boy as we all did.

Eventually, we placed Dougie in a hospital in Faribault, Minnesota, that cared for children with disabilities. We knew he would get the best care there, but it was very hard, terribly hard to leave him. We visited him as frequently as possible, but sadly he died in 1964.

We also lost our last child, Christopher, who died within hours of his birth as a result of problems related to a Eva Mae's pregnancy that prompted an emergency cesarean section.

We have six other children: Greg, Judi, Elizabeth (Beth), Paula, Steve, and Carol. All our children are treasures in our lives. I appreciate each and every one of them and my 11 grandchildren.

Eva Mae was a tremendous mother and wife. We were able to weather difficult times because of her strength and resilience. We really worked together as a team, she and I. Our faith also was a comfort to us in dealing with our grief of losing two children—our first and our last born.

Our family loved to visit Dougie at Faribault State Hospital as often as possible. *Back row from left:* me, Dougie, and Eva Mae holding Paula; *front row:* Greg, Elizabeth, and Judi.

Our growing family in 1966. Eva Mae and I loved this photo so much that we made it our Christmas card. *From left:* Carol, Steven, Paula, Elizabeth, Judi, Greg, Eva Mae, and me. Our dog Ginger is in front. Eva Mae made all our sweaters, except for her own!

Here is my family in 2008. *Back row from left:* Judi, Steven, Greg, and Carol. *Middle row from left:* Elizabeth and Paula. In front are Eva Mae and me.

CHAPTER EIGHT

Why Do We Fight Wars?

I have always been impressed with the speech President Franklin Roosevelt was supposed to give on January 11, 1945, the day before he died, as part of Jefferson Day remembrances across the country.[37]

> *Americans are gathered together this evening in communities all over the country to pay tribute to the living memory of Thomas Jefferson—one of the greatest of all democrats; and I want to make it clear that I am spelling that word "democrats" with a small "d."*
>
> *I wish I had the power, just for this evening, to be present at all of these gatherings.*
>
> *In this historic year, more than ever before, we do well to consider the character of Thomas Jefferson as an American citizen of the world.*
>
> *As Minister to France, then as our third President, Jefferson was instrumental in the establishment of the United States as a vital factor in international affairs.*
>
> *It was he who first sent our Navy into far-distant waters to defend our rights. And the promulgation of the Monroe Doctrine was the logical development of Jefferson's far-seeing foreign policy.*

Today this nation, which Jefferson helped so greatly to build, is playing a tremendous part in the battle for the rights of man all over the world.

Today we are part of the vast Allied force—a force composed of flesh and blood and steel and spirit—which is today destroying the makers of war, the breeders of hate in Europe, and in Asia.

In Jefferson's time our Navy consisted of only a handful of frigates—but that tiny navy taught nations across the Atlantic that piracy in the Mediterranean—acts of aggression against peaceful commerce and the enslavement of their crew—was one of the things which, among neighbors, simply was not done.

Today we have learned in the agony of war that great power involves great responsibility. Today we can no more escape the consequences of German and Japanese aggression than we could avoid the consequences of attacks by the Barbary corsairs a century and a half before.

We, as Americans, do not choose to deny our responsibility.

Nor do we intend to abandon our determination that, within the lives of our children and our children's children, there will not be a third world war.

We seek peace—enduring peace. More than an end to war, we want an end to the beginnings of all wars—yes, an end to this brutal, inhuman, and thoroughly impractical method of settling the differences between governments.

The once powerful, malignant Nazi state is crumbling; the Japanese war lords are receiving in their own homeland, the retribution for which they asked when they attacked Pearl Harbor.

But the mere conquest of our enemies is not enough.

We must go on to do all in our power to conquer the doubts and the fears, the ignorance and the greed, which made this horror possible.

Thomas Jefferson, himself a distinguished scientist, once spoke of the "brotherly spirit of science, which unites into one family all its votaries of whatever grade and however widely dispersed throughout the different quarters of the globe."

Today, science has brought all the different quarters of the globe so close together that it is impossible to isolate them one from another.

Today we are faced with the preeminent fact that, if civilization is to survive, we must cultivate the science of human relationships—the ability of all peoples, of all kinds, to live together and work together, in the same world, at peace.

Let me assure you that my hand is the steadier for the work that is to be done, that I move more firmly into the task, knowing that you—millions and millions of you—are joined with me in the resolve to make this work endure.

The work, my friends, is peace, more than an end of this war—an end to the beginning of all wars, yes, an end, forever, to this impractical, unrealistic settlement of the differences between governments by the mass killing of peoples.

Today as we move against the terrible scourge of war—as we go forward toward the greatest contribution that any generation of human beings can make in this world—the contribution of lasting peace—I ask you to keep up your faith. I measure the sound, solid achievement that can be made at this time by the straight edge of your own confidence and your resolve. And to you, and to all Americans who dedicate themselves with us to the making of an abiding peace, I say:

The only limit to our realization of tomorrow will be our doubts of today. Let us move forward with strong and active faith.

So many men came out of World War II with what we now called post-traumatic stress disorder, but what was called battle fatigue in my day and shell shock during World War I. These were often infantrymen like my roommate and brother Wally whom I call late casualties—not from their physical wounds but the emotional ones that we can't see. You would expect those who had seen slaughter in battle to suffer. But you couldn't readily see the internal battles that occurred among men after being in battle.

Some of those who liberated concentration camps reported lifelong trauma associated with what they saw. I have not, although on evenings when I've spoken to groups or shared the photos we took at Ohrdruf, I can practically smell the odors of those camps. Then, I have trouble falling asleep as my mind races with these memories.

War itself is so brutal and inhuman, something I saw in field hospitals. I got a bit hardened to those wounds of war after awhile and felt gratitude that I was not put in a position to have to slaughter enemy soldiers or be slaughtered myself. It affects people in different ways.

Like so many veterans and Holocaust survivors, I didn't talk much about my experiences in the war for decades, certainly not deeply. I wanted to put them behind me and move on with my life, my career, and family.

But after the 50th anniversary of D-Day in June 1994, we veterans were encouraged to talk about our experiences. I had retired from Sentry Insurance in 1984 as Director of Operations Human Resources. I had time to speak to school groups, businesses, and service clubs. I wanted people to know what had really happened, particularly in the face of those who denied the Holocaust occurred or suggested it was not so severe. I saw the impact of the evil done by the Nazis with my own eyes. I know how bad it was and didn't want the world to repeat those horrors.

I also revisited Omaha Beach in Normandy in July 2005, seeing the WWII landing beaches where some 2,200 Americans died and hundreds more were wounded in fighting to reach the high ground above. Most of these men were buried in the American Cemetery near Omaha Beach.

About once a year my business with Sentry took me to New Jersey, not far from where Colonel Sandford practiced medicine in Caldwell after the war. We spoke periodically by phone if I happened to be in New Jersey on business and had a free evening. After retirement, we talked periodically from home. I was so honored to learn that Sandy left the instruction to his son to call me after his death to let me know. Fred had already passed away by then, or he also would have gotten that sad call.

Fred and I had a mini reunion with Sandy in Milwaukee, Wisconsin, in 1996. He had a son who is a microbiologist at Johns Hopkins University in Baltimore, Maryland, but had been hired by the Medical College of Wisconsin to do research there.

The respect and friendship we felt during our time in World War II continued decades later. It was interesting to have these conversations about what we saw and experienced.

In my wartime diary, I was pretty harsh about the German people and questioned whether Germany could ever be included among civilized nations again. Most of us who served in the war or in the occupation questioned the willingness of the U.S. government to rebuild Germany and Japan after the

From left: Fred Kercheval, Col. Sandy, and me at our 1996 reunion.

war through the Marshall Plan, which was created by General George C. Marshall.

But as I reflected over time, I realized it was the wise thing to do, considering the seeds of World War II were planted by keeping German on its knees after World War I by the retribution that was part of the Treaty of Versailles. I do not excuse Germany in any way for what it did under Hitler, but recognize total destruction of any country has lasting ramifications.

The generation of German leaders who followed the Nazis was different, insisting that the country take responsibility for what it did. Initially, there was such shame about places like Dachau and Buchenwald that they did not want these places to exist, let alone become museum places to study hate and injustice. Now many German children are taken there to learn about the horrors of the Nazis.

Since the war I've twice visited Dachau Concentration Camp, one of 180 slave labor camps in Germany alone. It is still so hard to understand how humans can do to other human beings what we would consider to be inhumane to animals. Life was so cheap in those hellholes.

In my career and personal life, I have met many fine German people, including young folks who have come to the United States in high school and college exchanges, as well as business learning opportunities at Sentry Insurance. We have developed wonderful friendships that have continued far beyond our visits.

The final measures of whether the Marshall Plan and the various connections we've made with Germany—and Japan—were the right things to do are in our relationships. They now are among our closest allies.

Honors for My Service

I received an honor in 2002 from the French government for my service during World War II. Dominique Decherf, consul General for the French Consulate in Chicago, presented a certificate of appreciation in Madison, Wisconsin, to a bunch of us veterans from the European Theater. "It is a pleasure to in-

Page 10 Portage County Gazette March 15, 2013

Regnier recalls first liberated Nazi labor camp

By GENE KEMMETER
of The Gazette

John Regnier of Whiting said he still vividly recalls his most memorable experience from his days in the U.S. Army during World War II – going through the first slave labor camp that was liberated by U.S. soldiers in Germany.

Regnier told his story last year during a presentation at Sentry Insurance and recounted it Monday, March 11, for the Stevens Point Area Retired Teachers' Association at the Sky Club in Plover.

He also related his comments on seeing the concentration camp in a documentary that was shown on Wisconsin Public Television (WPT) in November 2003. The program, "Wisconsin WWII Stories Part II: Europe," was a partnership of the Wisconsin Historical Society and WPT, in association with the Wisconsin Department of Veterans Affairs. Regnier was one of 18 veterans interviewed for the segment.

Regnier was the supply sergeant for the 182nd Medical Battalion, which was supporting the 4th Armored Division during the Third Army's drive across France and Germany.

The battalion headquarters was in a convoy on April 12, 1945, when its commander noticed a group of soldiers gathering along-

John Regnier, a retired Sentry Insurance executive (left), recently talked about going through the first slave labor camp in Nazi Germany that was liberated by U.S. soldiers near the end of World War II. With him, from left, are his daughter, Carol Okray; granddaughter, Stacy Regnier; son, Steven Regnier; and grandson, Justin Regnier. (Portage County Gazette photo)

ly arrived at the camp and had enough strength left to take part, served as guides for Eisenhower's tour, Regnier said.

"When the MP (military policeman)

The photographer also developed his film, Regnier said, and they exchanged copies of the photos they had taken.

One of the photos the photographer had

John Regnier of Whiting (center) met Polish refugees in Germany after the end of World War II. Franz (left) lost his leg blow the knee when an artillery shell struck his home where he was hiding with his mother and father. His father was killed. Regnier arranged for Franz to receive a prosthesis from American forces. (John Regnier photo)

for the boy to wear. "It was one of the more

Speaking out about what I saw has become very important to me.

form you that you will be awarded the 'Thank You America Certificate from the French Government for your contribution to the liberation of France during World War II. France has never forgotten the sacrifice made by all of our Allies and wants to recognize your brave action."

The city of Stevens Point along with the Wisconsin Department of Veterans Affairs presented me with a Service to America Certificate of Appreciation in 2004. The citation read, "In solemn recognition of the sacrifices and leadership of men and women of the 'Greatest Generation.' In fighting to preserve a society you won the war, built the peace, and gave to future generations the precious gift of freedom. As the national monument to your World War II service is dedicated in Washington, your fellow citizens honor you. We pledge that your heroic achievements, commitment to freedom, and leadership of your comrades will not be forgotten."

In my mind, there were only two justified wars:

- The Civil War to end slavery and preserve the union.
- World War II, where we freed people from the most heinous of dictators.

War is a horrible way to solve problems, something I've come to believe more and more. No one who has seen the human carnage of war up close would be as eager as the chicken hawks—those who have never gone to war themselves—to send someone else's kids to war. War should never be a first resort, as men like former Vice President Dick Cheney seem to want it to be.

I'm offended by those who describe a soldier killed in a war "as willing to die for his country." We sign up for military service because we believe in our country, but we don't want to die for it. We do recognize dying is a risk that comes with being a soldier. But there is a big difference between being willing and accepting the risk.

Even General Patton once said, "No bastard ever won a war by dying for his country. He won it by making the other poor dumb bastard die for his country."

Sixty years after my own Christmas Eve at war, I spoke at my church in Stevens Point, Wisconsin, about my experience of celebrating Christmas Mass in 1944 at the beginning of the Battle of the Bulge in Arlon, Belgium. I quoted from my war diary and shared my concern for soldiers who were at war in the 21st Century the way I was at Christmas in 1944.

> *Tonight, December 24, 2004, the United States is involved in a war. Many young people of this country are doing what young people have done in Christmases in the past—fighting in a foreign land.*
>
> *I'd like to share with you for a few minutes my story of a Christmas in a foreign land, during wartime, 60 years ago.*
>
> *The entry in my diary for December 22, 1944, reads: "4th Armored Division expected to break into Bastogne any day. German defense fantastic. Supplies dropped by air. Surgical teams towed in the gliders. Many wounded in Bastogne. German dead piled up like cordwood around Bastogne. Bastogne almost completely leveled. 624th Clearing Co. and 467th Collecting Co. attached to us now. Outlook not very good for Christmas. Air forces out in strength as weather has cleared. Constant roar all day."*
>
> *It was in the early days of the Battle of the Bulge. The German armies had unleashed a surprise, massive counteroffensive in the Ardennes region of eastern Belgium a few days before Christmas. They quickly overran a rather new American Division taking about 8,000 American soldiers prisoner and killing many more. Bastogne was cut off and surrounded by the German army. The 3rd Army was in northern France preparing*

I spoke at the Newman Parish in Stevens Point, Wisconsin, in 2004, about Christmas 1944 in Arlon, Belgium, on the 60th anniversary of that moving experience. A few months after this book comes out, we will observe the 70th anniversary of that wartime Christmas Mass. It is hard to believe that much time has passed.

to invade Germany when this counter attack took place. The entire army received orders to move north into Luxemburg and Belgium.

On December 19 and 20th our Battalion was a part of the approximately 200,000 3rd Army troops who made this move. The winter weather was extremely severe. This, plus the great anxiety and stress of moving into a very dangerous war zone, did not permit a great deal of thought about the fast-approaching Christmas season.

We had moved into a vacated hospital building in Arlon, Belgium, a short distance out of Bastogne, to provide medical support for the 4th Armored Division. Their assignment was to liberate the American forces surrounded in Bastogne. We were all on high alert night and day as many German SS troops had taken American soldiers' uniforms from dead GIs. Disguised as American soldiers they had infiltrated into the American combat zone.

On Christmas morning we were told that an Army Chaplain would be celebrating Mass in the Arlon Cathedral for all 3rd Army soldiers in the area. This announcement was a very welcome and unanticipated opportunity to attend Mass. It's difficult to describe the feelings that we had as we entered this large, old church, It was packed wall to wall, standing room only, with fellow American soldiers in full battle gear. Other than an occasional burst of artillery fire overhead, we were in an oasis of total quiet and peace. I'm sure none of that group of soldiers will ever forget the overall tone and spiritual atmosphere as we celebrated this Mass in the midst of the war. This celebration was followed with a short communal penance service for the hundreds of GIs packed in the church.

This Christmas Mass on December 25, 1944, in the cathedral in Arlon, Belgium, has become the most memorable Mass that I have ever attended.

As we quietly left that very unique spiritual experience, each one of us was aware of what the words "Peace on Earth" really mean. And each one of us was only too aware of what it meant to return to fear, anxiety, and hellish human and material carnage of war. The Battle of the Bulge raged for about another six weeks and was the costliest single land battle of World War II. The U.S. lost 19,000 killed and 61,000 wounded. Germany lost 120,000 killed and unknown numbers were wounded.

Today, in another foreign land, many of our young people are fighting in another war, and we here are still praying for them and for Peace on Earth. My prayer this Christmas Eve is that world leaders will ever strive to value diplomacy and the lessons of history rather than rush to military solutions as the primary option of settling world conflicts.

Those words are as true today in 2014 as they were in 2004 and 1944. Today we fight the so-called War on Terrorism. The embryo of terrorist warfare goes back to the Nazis, who used torture, mass killings, and public executions as forms of terror to keep the populations they controlled in line.

It is my hope with this book to remind people once again of the horrors of war and of the kind of nationalism and racism that so often brings the world fighting. We must work as hard for peace as we do in war, as President Roosevelt said in that undelivered speech: "The work, my friends, is peace, more than an end of this war—an end to the beginning of all wars, yes, an end, forever, to this impractical, unrealistic settlement of the differences between governments by the mass killing of peoples."

Afterword

By Susan T. Hessel

In writing this book, my life has turned 180 degrees from the day in Sunday School at United Hebrew Temple in St. Louis, Missouri, when our class was forced to watch films of concentration/death/slave labor camp liberations.

When I turned away from the horrors I saw as a 12-year-old in the early 1960s, my teacher got right up into my face and said, "Why are you looking away? Those are all Jews, you know."

I was scared, tormented by what I saw. That more than anything turned me off to learning anything more about the Holocaust.

Also, there was much more to how very wrong what happened was than the fact that they—and I—were Jewish. The wiser comment from that teacher would have been, "Those are all humans, you know."

That is the point of this. It is true that Jews were the most targeted, and more died in these camps than people of other faiths, but we are all people.

Five decades or so later I had the opportunity to co-write

Susan T. Hessel is a personal historian dedicated to preserving life stories of individuals. A board member of the Association of Personal Historians, she is especially honored to work with those who have stood up in the face of repression and adversity.

a book about Dora Russek, an Auschwitz survivor. At first I said no, I didn't want to do that. But I later changed my mind and am so grateful that I did. I now cannot stop reading books and seeing films about World War II. There is so much to learn about it in trying to understand what cannot be understood.

In 2012, I had the opportunity to work on a book with Mary Rostad, who as a Catholic teenager during World War II fought back against the Nazis in any way she could when they occupied Brussels. She did all sorts of things that she admitted were absolutely crazy and risked her life and her family.

I wrote this book because it needed to be written, especially for young people who need to know it is worthwhile to fight against injustice when they see it in their lives. Young people need to see role models like Mary, Dora, and John.

It was an honor when Viterbo University published the book I co-wrote with Mary shortly before her death. *Squirrel Is Alive: A Teenager in the Belgian Resistance and French Underground* came out in 2012, thanks to the commitment of Darryle Clott, who is a Holocaust educator extraordinaire, and Richard Kyte, director of Viterbo's D.B. Reinhart Institute for Ethics in Leadership.

Regarding this just completed book, I am especially grateful for the early interview that Sean Van Domelen did with John. The fact that Sean, who has no immediate connection to the Holocaust, would do this is inspiring. I'm sure he has a great future ahead of him as an historian.

Denying the Deniers needed to be written to counter the

Holocaust deniers who shout their lies from platforms on television, on the Internet, and in newspapers and other publications. As a former newspaper reporter, I always sought out both sides of an argument. But as this book demonstrates, there aren't two sides in a discussion of the Holocaust, other than the causes leading up to it. There can be no debate about what happened. Deniers may yell loudly but their claims are simply not borne out by the facts. Deniers' claims are lies born of hate, just as the Holocaust was born of hate.

Thankfully, we still have witnesses whose stories put those lies to shame. John began this book with General Eisenhower's words about this after touring that first camp. They bear repeating:

> *The things I saw beggar description. . . . The visual evidence and the verbal testimony of starvation, cruelty, and bestiality were so overpowering as to leave me a bit sick. In one room, where there were piled 20 to 30 naked men killed by starvation, General Patton would not even enter. He said he would get sick if he did so. I made the visit deliberately, in order to be in a position to give firsthand evidence of these things if ever, in the future, there develops a tendency to charge these allegations* merely to propoganda.

1. Gen. Dwight D. Eisenhower, Letter to Chief of Staff George Marshall, April 12, 1945.

2. Gen. Dwight D. Eisenhower, Letter to Chief of Staff George Marshall, April 12, 1945.

3. Technical Sergeant John Regnier, letter home to family, April 16, 1945.

4. "Ex-Legislator Emil Regnier Dies at 78," *Minneapolis Star Tribune,* June 4, 1980.

5. "Okie Migrations," Oklahoma Historical Society Encyclopedia of Oklahoma History and Culture, "http://digital.library.okstate.edu/encyclopedia/entries/o/ok008.html

6. http://www.measuringworth.com/uscompare/relativevalue.php

7. http://www.campforrest.com/brief_look_camp_forrest.htm

8. "United States Army Interment Camps: Camp Forrest, Tennessee, http://www.gaic.info/camp_usarmy.htm

9. Camp Shanks World War II museum, http://www.hudsonrivervalley.com/Details.aspx?sid=c5a8c9f0-fa2d-4e53-8fad-dfe0124188c4

10. http://www.qmfound.com/history_of_rations.htm

11. http://westwall.elvamie.nl/en/data/archive/breakingsiegfriedline.html

12. "Battle of the Bulge: Overview of the Battle," http://www.army.mil/botb/overview.html

13. Brian M. Solbel, *The Fighting Pattons,* 1997.

14. "The Battle of the Bulge," http://www.history.army.mil/html/reference/bulge/index.html

15. Battle of the Bulge: Overview of the Battle," http://www.army.mil/botb/overview.html

16. Bethanne Kelly Patrick, Military.com, "Gen. Anthony Mcauliffe," http://www.military.com/Content/MoreContent?file=ML_mcauliffe_bkp

17. Battle of the Bulge: Overview of the Battle," http://www.army.mil/botb/overview.html.

18. "Life at the Battle of the Bulge: Photos from Hitler's Last Gamble," http://life.time.com/history/battle-of-the-bulge-life-photos-from-hitlers-last-gamble-1944-1945/#1

19. Reuel Long, "Remembering Another Enemy: Cold Weather," www.battleofthebulgememories.be/stories26/32-battle-of-the-bulge-us-army/730-remembering-another-enemy-cold-weather.html

20. Edward R. Murrow's Report from Buchenwald, http://www.jewishgen.org/ForgottenCamps/Witnesses/MurrowEng.html

21. U.S. Policy During WWII: U.S. Army & the Holocaust, http://www.jewishvirtuallibrary.org/jsource/Holocaust/usarmy_holo.html

22. http://www.americancenturies.mass.edu/centapp/oh/story.do?shortName=cohen1945

23. http://furtherglory.wordpress.com/2011/12/04/who-was-general-eisenhowers-interpreter-when-he-visited-ohrdruf/

24. http://ohrdruf.simmins.org

25. Ohrdruf, Holocaust Encyclopedia, U.S. Holocaust Memorial Museum website, www.uuhmm.org

26. U.S. Policy During WWII: U.S. Army & the Holocaust, http://www.jewishvirtuallibrary.org/jsource/Holocaust/usarmy_holo.html

27. Ohrdruf, Holocaust Encyclopedia, U.S. Holocaust Memorial Museum, http://www.ushmm.org/wlc/en/article.php

?ModuleId=10006131

28. Franklin D. Roosevelt, speech given on 50th anniversary of Mayo Clinic, August 8, 1934.

29. Ebensee (Austria), http://www.jewishvirtuallibrary.org/jsource/Holocaust/ebensee.html

30. David Housset, *The Other Kingdom,* 1947, p. 29.

31. The Treatment of Soviet POWs: Starvation, Disease, and Shootings, June 1941–January 1942, U.S. Holocaust Memorial Museum, http://www.ushmm.org/wlc/en/article.php?ModuleId=10007183

32. Ted Paluch, Malmedy Massacre Survivor, Oral History Spotlight, News from the National WWII Museum. http://www.nww2m.com/2012/12/oral-history-spotlight-ted-paluch-malmedy-massacre-survivor/

33. Pierre Moulin, *Dachau, Holocaust and U.S. Samurais,* 2007

34. Kevin Freking, "Japanese-American World War II Vets honored by Congress," , November 2, 2011, http://www.nbcnews.com/id/45141156/ns/us_news-life/t/japanese-american-wwii-vets-honored-congress/#.UhTmcBaRCeE

35. "The GI Bill's History: Born of Controversy: The GI Bill of Rights," Department of Veterans Affairs, http://www.gibill.va.gov/benefits/history_timeline/

36. Timy Brady, "A History of Student Health," July-August 2006, Univeristy of Minnesota Alumni Association.

37. Franklin D. Roosevelt: "Undelivered Address Prepared for Jefferson Day.," April 13, 1945. Online by Gerhard Peters and John T. Woolley, The American Presidency Project, http://www.presidency.ucsb.edu/ws/?pid=16602.

DISCUSSION QUESTIONS

1. What was the Holocaust?
2. What did John Regnier actually see?
3. Was he a hero? Why or why not?
4. Why do you think he waited so long to talk about his experience?
5. Is this story important? Why or why not?
6. What would you say to people who say the Holocaust did not happen or was much less severe than it is portrayed?

Made in United States
North Haven, CT
17 January 2026

86881205R00141